The Business of Family Business

Mirza Yawar Baig

Text copyright © Mirza Yawar Baig 2017
Cover photo copyright © Mirza Yawar Baig 2017

This book is sold subject to the condition that it shall not, by way of trade or otherwise, be lent, resold, hired out, or otherwise circulated without prior written consent of Mirza Yawar Baig, in any form of binding or cover other than that in which it is published and without a similar condition including this condition being imposed on the subsequent purchaser and without limiting the rights under copyright reserved above, no part of this publication maybe reproduced, stored in or introduced into a retrieval system or transmitted in any form or by any means (electronic, mechanical, photocopying, recording or otherwise) without the permission of the copyright owner.

Table of Contents

FOREWORD 4

ABOUT THIS BOOK 7

IT ALL BEGINS IN THE MIND 12

CULTURE AND THE FAMILY 38

ENDURING LEADERSHIP™ 87

ORGANIZATIONAL EXCELLENCE MODEL 87

ENDURING LEADERSHIP™ 151

INDIVIDUAL EXCELLENCE MODEL 151

KEEPING THE FAMILY TOGETHER WHILE TRANSFORMING THE BUSINESS.. 183

WHEN 'FAMILY' MEANS SOMEONE ELSE 217

ACKNOWLEDGEMENTS & CONCLUDING NOTES 236

Foreword

The last five decades have seen many family businesses becoming extinct or becoming endangered. The odds of a family business going into a third generation have become a rare occurrence, amidst the many changes taking place in the business world. The most significant has been the shorter product life cycles and traditional industries run by families being replaced by large corporations. As a result the family companies are challenged to re-invent themselves over and over in order to be competitive.

We were under the impression that complications and challenges in running a family business were unique to us until we met Yawar and read his book "Business of Family Business". The emotional attachment to business succession, children coming into business.... all these are observed in family businesses no matter where they come from.

Hence the book became part of us and it was certainly a Golden Scroll and definitely a cut above the rest! It provides clear and practical tools that could be used not only in a family business but in any company! We have enthusiastically applied the concepts within our business and have been happy to see positive results. The concepts helped us immensely in our journey in making the company change from a people led to a process led institution.
Yawar works with us closely to help us instill these concepts and his flexibility and deep understanding of the intricacies in managing family business, makes life easy for all of us to forge ahead, in making the much needed changes, ensuring

longevityand success of the business. Undoubtedly, he preaches through experience and does walk the talk!

The Family Firm Institute–Goodman Longevity Study, released last year, suggests that family business leaders, advisors and academics "reframe the dialogue on succession and longevity." In this light Yawar's book would be a must read to management practitioners. The book is a structured presentation of the rich experience of Yawar Baig in a meaningful way, providing practical tools to any management practitioner in a family business or otherwise.

Hanif Yusoof
Group CEO – Expolanka Holdings Limited
Founder Member of the business

About this Book

When a caterpillar looks in the mirror it does not see a butterfly. Yet hidden in that form is the potential to take the epitome of sluggishness and transform it into the epitome of grace, lightness and flight. The only condition is that the very nature of the thing must change completely. Caterpillars have no choice in the matter. People and businesses do. And therein lies the trap. The trap to remain the way you are, eating leaves and grass, crawling from place to place and thereby miss the opportunity to eat nectar and fly from flower to flower at will. Why would someone choose to be a caterpillar over being a butterfly? Because the status quo is always more comfortable and after all, when you look in the mirror, you only see a caterpillar!!

Family businesses need a similar transformation if they seriously intend to become global players in the world market. A transformation that is intrinsic, primordial, intense and painful but which then opens the doors into a world that you did not even know, exists. A world of global influence, great wealth and power and the potential to leave behind a legacy that lives on long after the founders have gone the way of all life. The choice is ours. It is not an easy choice. It is not a quick fix transformation that will happen without serious effort. It is not a course of action that will not meet opposition from other caterpillars. However as I said, the choice is ours to make.

Once the choice is made, then there are ways to make it happen and that is what this book is about. It is about showing the 'How' to those who know the 'Why'. If you have not made the choice yet, by all means read the book – I need to sell the book – but believe me, it will not do you much good.

The intention is the measure of the action and without a clear intention and determination to walk the path of transformation, nothing will happen. Nothing significant or worth talking about.

I have seen too many business families claiming that they want to make the transformation from being Person-led to Process-driven and then failing to take the tough calls. So I will not fool you or myself. I can show you how. I can't make you do it nor can I do it for you just as the doctor can't eat the medicine on your behalf. So do ask the questions to yourself and convince yourself that you do want to take the step to begin and sustain the transformation and then read this book. The process of transformation that I have suggested in tried and tested and it works; provided the will to make it work is there. Without that will the show of making the transformation will eventually do more harm than good because the pretense at transforming destroys credibility and enthusiasm that is impossible to regain. As I said, the choice is ours to make.

The Caterpillar and the Butterfly
The contrasts are stark. Almost diametrically opposite. That is why the transformation is not easy and not quick. Nor is it painless. But as in the analogy, it is possible and will happen provided serious sustained effort is put into it. To give you an idea of what I am talking about I have listed and compared the socio-psychological factors that differentiate family owned and operated businesses from process driven organizations. This is not an exhaustive list and you may well find factors that you can add.

However it does suffice to underline the differences and to show clearly how opposed these factors are to one another. I don't wonder that the vast number of family businesses never make the critical transition from Person-led to Process-driven. I marvel at the ones that do. The transformation is not easy. But then nothing worth doing is easy, is it? What is important is to realize, is that if you do take the decision to do what it takes to ensure that the business you started or inherited outlasts you, then it can be done. But that the change begins with you. For only the one who wants to change can decide to change. All change begins with the individual.

I have drawn on my own experience of having worked in one of the largest family businesses in India, the Murugappa Group (Turnover $3 billion, 25+ companies, established in 1900) for a period of 10 years. During the course of this period, for a variety of reasons, I developed close personal friendships with several family members including the patriarch Mr. A.M.M.Arunachalam who along with his brothers was a member of the Founding Group. He and his wife were kind enough to spend a lot of time with my wife and I and told us the entire history of their family and the business, not from the perspective of story-tellers but from the perspective of the history-makers. The fact that I speak Tamil fluently helped as they were both very comfortable talking about their life and its challenges in their own language. This gave me a very deep insight into the complex, often 'mysterious' reasons why family business owners take some decisions, especially in our Asian/Middle Eastern cultures. I am most grateful to him and others in that family for this privilege. I couldn't have wished for more qualified teachers.

In addition to this I draw upon my consulting experience with several other business families in India, Sri Lanka, Saudi Arabia, Britain and South Africa over the past 28 years which has given me excellent insights into what makes family businesses succeed or fail. What I have mentioned here has reference to family businesses in Asia, Africa and the Middle East, though I dare say the principles apply to businesses elsewhere. Cultural factors also relate to this region. It is my hope that those who read this will find it useful and that it will generate healthy dialogue leading to lessons which all of us can benefit from.

In the interest of ease of reading I have not attempted to say 'her' everywhere I have said 'him'. But let me make it absolutely clear that entrepreneurship is not gender specific. What a man can do, a woman can also do and often better and with greater sensitivity and care. So please do read 'him/her' at every 'him'. So also when I have said 'founder' this can mean an individual or a small 'founding group' as is seen in several cases.

I have reflected on and described what it takes to build leadership and create successors who can carry forward the legacy we worked all our lives to create. I call this process, building **'Enduring Leadership©'**. Leadership that will endure long after we have gone.

If followed and implemented well this method will result in the creation of winning cultures that will ensure that the vision outlasts the visionary and continues to inspire others. I have tried to stay with my own experience in helping organizations conceptualize and implement the **Enduring Leadership©** Model and have also cited some examples from sources other than my own experience which lead me to believe that my experience isborne out by others who have had similar success. I have also tried to briefly outline the implementation strategy for this model for anyone who would like to give it a try.

Mirza Yawar Baig

IT ALL BEGINS IN THE MIND

'In the beginning was the thought. It then focused on material and created the plan. The plan manifested itself into a working model. The model asked, "What happens after me?" The intellect answered, "That depends on what you want to happen. Seek to give and so you will get. Seek to take and it will be taken from you. And the rest is history."

The Critical Mindset Change from <u>Consumption to Contribution</u>

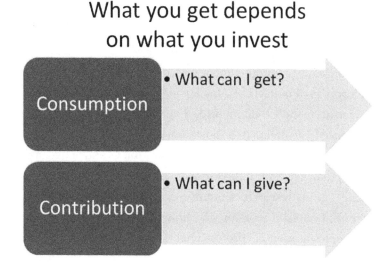

"It is important to ask yourself why you do what you do. Because it is the why that drives the what. 'Why' is the purpose. 'What' is the method. The purpose determines the method, because the purpose looks at the result it seeks to create. In business and in life, if you approach someone or some situation one way, you see it from one perspective. You approach the same person or situation another way you see a very different picture. So what you see depends on how you approach what you do. So always ask yourself why, before you embark on the what."

So why do you do business?
If you ask many entrepreneurs this question you get many different answers. Some say, 'To make money.' Some say, 'To build an organization.' Some say, 'To become wealthy.'

In my view the most powerful reason to do business is to serve humanity. I say it is the most powerful reason because if you do business for this reason, all the other reasons; making money, becoming wealthy, building an organization; will be accomplished automatically. In addition you will leave behind a legacy that will spread goodness long after you are gone. Money is a consequence of intelligent effort. Accumulating money is not a worthy goal in itself. Today business people are the single most powerful force in the world. Every other kind of person is influenced by them. It is business which funds politicians and government, influences government policy and law making, conceptualizes and builds major infrastructure projects, pays armies, funds research, sets up universities and builds hospitals, schools, houses of worship and homes. No other single grouping of people, academia, professional, scientific, religious, political; has the same collective power to act to influence and shape society.

The East India Company, as a business house ruled India for 100 years on its own and reshaped the nation, destroyed local industry, annexed independent nations and extended its rule from its board room in London, long before the British government came on the scene. The story of the Dutch in the East Indies and Southern Africa is similar in the nature of the way it conquered the land, destroyed local African populations and changed the world for ever. Business runs the world, but often for the wrong reason, which is profit. So it tends to sacrifice long term goals for short term influence. It is not within the scope of this book to go into history in detail but it will be very interesting for anyone who wants to make the effort to read and imagine what the nature of nations would have been if the people who took those decisions had service instead of profit as their goal. The conclusion that the reader would inescapably come to, is that with service as its goal, profit would not only have been made but would have been made far more consistently and in far greater quantity. For the simple reason that strong economies of developed people are far better for commerce than economies being systematically bled dry to create good looking balance sheets. In the end the economy dies and the business dies with it. History is witness to this, and sadly to the fact that nations which don't learn from history are condemned to repeat it.

When you focus on serving, on influencing, on acquiring significance, money will follow. And it will follow in the best ways. Without exploiting anyone. When accumulating wealth and material things becomes the goal, then exploitation, sharp practice and wheeling and dealing often become accepted ways. Money is made, but in ways that lack honor, respectability or worth. Ways that make you rich at the expense of other's rights. People get very wealthy by dealing in arms, drugs and other commodities of death. They get rich by hoarding food in times of crisis and selling it for the highest price that they can get. They make profit. But with the profit come the tears of the hungry, the wails of the bereaved and the sigh of the helpless. Eyes are raised to the heavens and those who have no power on earth invoke the power of the creator of the earth, against those who deprived them of their rights. In my view that is a very expensive bargain.
So you must always ask why you are doing business. The most critical mindset change that one must make is to change one's focus from being oriented towards what you can get from the business to what you can give to the business. From consumption to contribution. From breaking up to building. In family

businesses this is often the most difficult thing to do. And the reason is that to take, is all that people have been taught.

In my experience many business families spend far too little time on the upbringing of their children especially in inculcating the value of contribution. Of each generation creating its own legacy and not being content to ride on the back of the earlier generation. They give their children the same education that is given to the children of ordinary people who they employ. They don't prepare their children for the distinctly different responsibility that they will have to shoulder. This is not about arrogance or about creating a new caste system. It is about merely recognizing the fact that the scions of business families are going to inherit power and wealth entirely out of context of their own effort. It is therefore essential for them to understand the distinctly different responsibility that comes with such wealth and power and for which they will be answerable to their families, their descendants and society at large.

They need a very different education, very different life experiences and very different criteria to measure themselves, all of which have to be inculcated from the earliest childhood. Being rich or poor is not about how much you have. It is about how you think. The best and most powerful asset that business founders can give to their descendants is to teach them these tools. Few do. That is why few family businesses survive into the 3rd and 4th generation. As mentioned earlier, in the East as few as 14% make it to the 4th generation. In the West, the number is even more dismal. The East benefits from some cultural advantages of strong families and religious ethos which the West lost more than a century ago.

I've met many founders who struggled very hard to set up and grow their business and who say to themselves (and to everyone else) with great feeling and tears in their eyes, "I will never allow my children to face the hardship that I had to go through." When I hear this statement I say to them, "Please change the wording. Say, 'I will never allow my children to build resilience, character and strength. I will never allow them to have the power that I have, to succeed.' Say this because in effect that is what you are really saying." For many of them this statement of mine is a shock. They had never thought about their view on upbringing of children in that light.

They equate expense with quality. They give their children the most expensive education which insulates them from the realities of life and so they never learn to fight the real battles. They give them the most expensive toys which in reality teach them to define human value in terms of material worth (the 'best' kids are those who have the best toys). They insulate them from poverty, deprivation, lack of resources and thereby they 'protect' them from being exposed to the power of drive, ambition, single minded focus on achieving big, ambitious, scary goals. They build walls between their children and the people who they must in the end, deal with. People who will one day, work in their organizations and decide their fate. People who need to be inspired, led, cared for and supported. And therefore people who must be understood. Not simply in order to do good and be charitable but because the success of the business and family depends on the development of these people; the great multitude. The fond parents forget or ignore the fact that one day the time will come for the soft little molly coddled pussy cat to enter the jungle of the real world without any of the tools it needs to survive, much less to lead others.

As was the practice of the kings of old, princes and princesses must be taught differently from ordinary people. A good way to understand this is to see how child prodigies are brought up. They are not given the same education as everyone else. The entire focus of their education, both formal and informal, is based on the eventual role that they must play. Only then can the true glory of the gift that they have been bestowed with, come forth. Children born to wealth have been gifted with resources. They are not ordinary children. To treat them as if they were is to deny them their opportunity to make a mark in the world that others will have to try far harder to do.

They must be brought up always with the final aim of leading a great business house in mind. They must be carefully watched, nurtured and mentored from the earliest age. They must be given tasks of graduated difficulty so that they learn to win on their own. They must be allowed to face their fears and to conquer them.

They must be supported but not protected. They must be advised but not told what to do. They must be allowed to take their own decisions but not without the benefit of the frame of reference of the value of honor, fairness, responsibility, accountability, nurturing and trusteeship. They must be allowed to feel, to cry in the night for the hardships that others undergo, to build friendships and relationships that span the boundaries of color, race, religion, nationality and much more difficult, social order and prejudice. They must learn that to be poor and to be honorable are not mutually exclusive; just as to be rich and to be honorable are not the same thing and don't happen automatically. They must learn that virtue is a state of mind. A stance, a decision, a position that one takes, not because someone is watching but because of one's own sense of one's identity.

I do because of who I am. And I become, because I do. They must learn that our actions define us. They must learn that people will define them on the basis of both what they owned and what they contributed. But they will honor them only for what they contributed. Because we are remembered, not for what we had but for what we gave. Only when they are taught to focus on contribution from their earliest childhood will they be able to fight the force of consumerism that is focused on consumption. Blind, self centered consumption that in the end will consume us all, if it is allowed to proliferate unchallenged. Business families must bring up children who will challenge these norms and create a society that is focused on contribution instead of consumption, so that in the end we leave behind a place that is the better for our passing.

It is when parents bring up self centered children focused on consumption, that when it comes to the business, they think nothing of breaking up both the business and the family in their fight to get the most for themselves. When children are focused to what they can contribute they will work to grow the business and to ensure that its influence and service is enjoyed by more and more people, worldwide. In the process it is inevitable that the family itself grows and becomes richer and more powerful because as I said, wealth and power are the result of intelligent effort. Not its objective.

Spoon feeding in the long run teaches us nothing but the shape of the spoon. ~E.M. Forster

The biggest mistake that parents make is not to define boundaries. Parents must parent. Many parents today seem to be too focused on being 'friends' to their children at the expense of parenting. In this endeavor they bend over backward trying to be nice to the children and basically do whatever the children want them to. Boundaries are therefore never firm and clear.

They are always open to negotiation and children push the boundaries until they get what they want from parents who have confused parenting with being 'friendly' per se. Parents must remember that their children can have many friends but they have only 2 parents. Parents have been assigned the role of parenting. Every other role is optional. The only assigned role is that of parenting and so they need to do that first and foremost.

Children are forever testing boundaries. So these must be clear. For example, that you can disagree with parents on issues provided you do it in the right way by being respectful and not cheeky. That cheekiness is not cute, it is insulting. That joking and insulting are two different things. That assertiveness is to insist on your rights without violating the rights of others. That aggressiveness is to violate the rights of others. One is commendable, the other is reprehensible. That caring for your environment (read: home, office, bathroom, car, garden, pets etc.) is your job and not the job of parents, or servants. Servants are supposed to clean the home once in a day. Not every time the child makes a mess. It is a common sight in the East, especially in wealthy family homes, to see the mother or a servant picking up after the child who is a moving litter creator. Children must learn that making a mess of the home or your own room is not acceptable. That your room is your own but not to do with or in as you please. That the rules of the home apply even inside your room. Children must be taught that meal times are sacred because the home is not a hotel where one can simply order room service. Meals, especially the one meal at which the whole family eats together, may not be missed or interrupted. Mealtime is for the family and any family guests. It is okay to invite friends to a meal at home but not okay to talk to them on the phone while the rest of the family eats. Children must learn that their guests must also follow the rules of the family home. That exams, games, TV shows, football, cricket or basketball matches and so on are not acceptable excuses for missing the family meal.

Naturally it is the parents who have to set the norm. If the father misses the meal without comment, then so will the child. If the father sits in front of the TV because he wants to see what happened to his favorite team and to be able to do that, moves the meal to the living room so that everyone eats mechanically with eyes glued to the screen, then this will become the norm and he will have no moral authority to insist that the children do something different. If parents sit in their favorite chair and shout out to the servant to get this or that, so will the children. If parents litter, children will too. If parents pay children to wash cars, mow lawns, clean attics or garages, instead of personally doing these things taking the children along with them, then children will learn that as long as they can throw money at some poor person to do their work, they need not care for their own environment. Not only will they not learn to take care of their common spaces but they will also learn to treat some jobs with disrespect and to look down on those who do those jobs.

Each of these things above can be linked to one or more of the evils of our society. A society that is stratified according to economic circumstances, not according to knowledge, moral values or being honorable. A society where people don't care for other people. Where the self is worshipped and indulgence is the supreme goal. Where freedom is defined as the ability to indulge your whims with impunity, even when some of this indulgence may be breaking the laws of God or country. Where the law is applied differently based on who has the money to circumvent it or to get out of trouble by paying their way. Where the ones who create the corruption by paying to get benefits out of turn, then turn around and whine about what a corrupt society we have. Where justice is denied to some because others pay 'speed money' to an 'educated' judge and then they complain about how corrupt the judiciary has become. Where the fact that the effect of one's own activity, speech or conduct may be infringing on the rights of others, is not even part of any discussion.

Children, especially of business families who come from high income homes must be taught the value of service. They must endure hardship and learn that for some people air-conditioning, cars, unlimited hot & cold running water, fridges bursting at the seams and clean sheets on a soft bed are not even novelties; because a novelty is something that you do have, even if only occasionally. But those people still live and laugh and play. Children must be taught the value of compassion, courage and service. They must be allowed to experience the joy of sharing. Of giving and then seeing the light of disbelieving delight in the eyes of the receiver. Nothing compares to the joy of giving something to someone who did not even dream of getting it. They must be taught that to give someone what you don't really want is still good but not as appreciable as giving away something that you love because someone else needs it more. This demonstrates genuine care and concern.

For example for a teenager to volunteer to spend time with old people (related or not) is to give away their time, which may not have any monetary value but which is something that is dear to young people. This and other such activities must be encouraged and appreciated. Not by giving money in exchange but by talking to the child and asking what they believe they gained from the action. It is only when they learn to take pleasure in the giving of itself that this giving becomes sustainable.

This is a power that is given in the hands of those who have resources, who actually hold the resources of others in trust, to be delivered on call, when they need it. Those who use these resources for themselves without any concern for others are really violating their trust for which they will be held accountable.

Children must be taught that value is not equal to cost. For example that the cost of learning may be negligible but the value of knowledge is immeasurable. And so the scholar must be respected and honored for his knowledge even if he is poor. That the muddy handprints of your little daughter may well have ruined your Armani suit when she rushed to give you a hug as you returned from work, but the value of the hug is far more than the value of the suit and so you keep silent and return her hug with a bigger one and add a kiss as a bonus. The suit can be cleaned or replaced. The broken heart of a little girl can't be repaired. Children must be taught that the mud and brick structure that they live in is a house, not a home. And no matter how big yours is, there is always another somewhere else which is bigger, shinier, taller, wider or more beautiful. How expensive or big it is, does not show how happy and contented are those who live in it. And it is this happiness and contentment that make the home, not mud and brick.

Possessions add cost, not value.
Children must be taught that humans have more intrinsic value than anything material which can be bought, sold or junked. That cars, branded clothing, watches, gadgets, material possessions, expensive houses don't add value to the people who use them. **Possessions add cost, not value.** Anyone sensible will seek to add value to himself, not cost. People who believe that possessions add value or seek to convince others of this, have no value for themselves. They have low self esteem and are seeking to lower the value of the human being. Children must be taught that a car, no matter how expensive, is transportation, not a symbol. Except of bad judgment which makes someone put huge amounts of money into a depreciating asset. A shirt is clothing, a watch is meant to tell the time and shoes are meant to walk in. None of these define you, are not statements, nor indicators of what kind of human being you are. It is your character, your actions, what you stand for, your principles and your values, which define you. Not what you possess. What you possess can be stolen or taken away from you. Your character, your values, your principles are the stuff of memories that you leave behind. By these you will be remembered, honorably or otherwise. Live a life such that you will be remembered with honor. Teach children these things by personal example. Because that is the only way to teach them.

Children must be taught the value of money. The value of earning it, of investing it, of making it earn for you. They must learn the difference between spending and investing. They must be trained to be wealth creators, not wealth spenders. They must be taught that spending is to incur an expense for something that can give no return but instead, itself depreciates in value. Investing is to incur an expense for something that gives a return on your investment. Children learn to handle money by actually handling money. So give them an allowance and then ask them to present monthly P&L accounts and an annual Balance Sheet. See what the headings are, under which they spent their allowance. See if they have found ways to make their allowance earn for them instead of simply spending it on consumables. Show them the alternatives they may have missed. Warren Buffet started trading when he was in his teens. When asked he said that his only regret was that he had not started earlier. Once children see how they will actually gain and have more money by this kind of thinking you have won. See if they spent some money on the welfare of others. Guide them by example. Teach them to be rich. For as I have said earlier, being rich or poor is a function of how you think. Not of what or how much you possess.

As we bring up our children, so we create the society we live in. We have succeeded in creating a society that is rich in resources and poor in the willingness to share. That is why we have hunger and poverty. Our society is rich in material and poor in morals and spirit. That is why we have evil and sin. Our society is rich in information but poor in wisdom. That is why the most 'educated' nations among us are the most barbaric. That is why we have people in some countries starving to death while in 2007-8 more than £ 1 billion worth of food was thrown away in Britain alone. Is this an issue of food production, distribution or simply of lack of concern for others?

We have created a society that has concentrated power and wealth in the hands of a few who have no concern for others. These are people who have the resources to actually create a world without hunger, educated, with proper medical care, where there are none homeless and which is free from crime. But instead they have created a world that has the capability of destroying itself 40 times over. Nobody stops to ask how this will happen the second time, let alone for another 38 times.

The correction has to begin at home
It is this self-centered thinking that has given rise to the so-called 'Rat Race'. It will not be out of place to share some thoughts and reflections on what the Rat Race is and how to beat it.

Genesis of the idea
A friend asked me to show him a way to get out of the rat race and on the spur of the moment I said, 'Become a cat.' Then I reflected on the qualities that a cat represents and those which a rat represents and I tried to see how these can help us to create life quality and satisfaction. What differentiates a rat from a cat? And how does that help us? That is what this is about. One word of caution; like all analogies this also ends at a point. The point being that this is meant for people, not rats or cats. So please don't get too stuck to the zoology and remain with the concept and philosophy of how we can power-up our lives.

Rat versus Cat
Now what distinguishes the Rat from the Cat? In my view it is focus that distinguishes the Rat in the Rat Race from the Cat which is watching from his perch.

In the Rat Race, the focus is self aggrandizement & destructive competition:
There is constant comparison with others. This produces dissatisfaction with one's own situation and so one strives harder to beat the other. Naturally this focus also produces the need to show off, because what is the use of gain if it can't be flaunted? People don't feel good because they have more, but because they

have more than others do. So if everyone had the same or similar, if everyone developed, the satisfaction would be less. One feels very satisfied not by being wealthy but by being <u>more wealthy</u> than one's friends, companions, family, and being able to show off that wealth so that others feel jealous, envious, frustrated. Since material things are easier to accumulate and display, the focus of the Rat Race is very materialistic. People build houses not to create warm and loving homes but to create edifices to their egos. They fill them with artifacts bought in antique stores that arrived there from the houses of other rats of times gone by, who also filled their houses with artifacts from the homes of still other rats gone by.

Little do they reflect on the irony of this. Cars for rats, are not transportation but statements of their position in society. Weddings are not about the young people starting a new life but an opportunity for the parents to flaunt their wealth. Victims of the Rat Race beg to be invited to such 'high society weddings' and then gaze with longing eyes at all that they are never likely to have and go home and complain about how wasteful the hosts were and in what bad taste their party was. This is because rat parties are not about meeting friends and feeling good, but about looking to see what others wore and feeling bad. That is why all the good feeling of wearing a nice dress or a good piece of jewelry becomes saw dust in the mouth the moment they see another person wearing a huge rock on a rope.

Aah!! And of course in the Rat Race there is a great deal of rejoicing in the misfortunes of others. Nothing is more satisfying than to talk about the robbery in someone's house in which they lost all their jewellery or the accident in which their Bentley was totaled. All this is of course spoken of in pained tones, but one only has to look into the eyes to see the undisguised glee in them. Rat societies are very uncaring places in which personal gain is the only consideration. Means fair or foul are not a matter of interest to anyone. Results justify the means. As long as I gain, it does not matter how I gained. It matters even less at whose expense I gained. Moral values, codes of behavior, principles, religion are all means to be used in gaining advantage over others. There is no real loyalty to any of these things. They are tools to be used, ruthlessly and without apology and to be cast aside when they are no longer useful. In the end, worship is only of the self and of personal desire.

Since accumulation of material possessions is essential to win in the Rat Race, rats become stingy and hoard resources. They won't share what they have with others because it will reduce their own store. Even when some things they have may be time sensitive and can get spoilt or redundant unless they are used, rats will still hoard them and will not give them to others or allow others to use their resources. Rats will also not share knowledge to ensure that others never have a chance to succeed. Rat societies are characterized by a lack of education and disparities in learning and capability. Safety becomes the key driver. Risk taking disappears. Fear of losing possessions dominates all thinking and various means are sought to prevent that. Security agencies do good business in rat societies. Rats are unwilling to face the fact that societies in which disparities between people are less or non-existent, crime automatically disappears. Rats don't like to face this fact because in order for disparities to disappear, wealthy rats must share their wealth. But this goes against the very grain of rat-ness especially since the source of all satisfaction is to see that others have less than you. So there is a vested interest in rat societies to ensure that disparities remain.

Interestingly this focus on the other, also produces complacency. When you have more than others and when everyone else is staring at you in envy, then there is no need to strive more. So enterprise dies once a certain amount of stuff has been accumulated as there is nobody left to impress or there is too much to protect. Real progress, be it in knowledge or power, stops as rats don't like to take risk. Risk is essential to stretch the boundaries of the known and explore ways of dealing with the unknown. Risk is essential to learn how much more one can achieve. But risk has within it, the possibility of failure. Since rats are afraid of failure as this can result in their losing some of their possessions they hate risk and constantly seek safety. So progress stops.

Since satisfaction comes only in comparison with others, rats in power are despotic and tyrannical. It is from seeing others kowtowing to them that they get a sense of wellbeing. Loyalty to the king rat becomes the primary virtue. Questioning of those in power or of whatever they stand for is the cardinal sin. Rat societies become inward looking and lose perspective and have no vision. The boundary between the ruler and the state disappears. The ruler says, "I am the state." Difference of opinion is seen as opposition and disagreement with or disapproval of those in power becomes treason. Rat societies equate the government with the country and disagreement with one is seen as disloyalty to the other. That is why in the Rat Race, even if you win, you are still a rat. Ask yourself: How many rats do you know? And is one of them the one you see in the mirror?

Now let us look at what it is to be a Cat.

The Cat is focused primarily on himself but unlike the rat the cat focuses on developing its skill as a hunter. Cats don't hoard, so every day is a new opportunity to hunt. To improve skills, to learn from previous mistakes, to take risk and pit one's own strengths and talents against external forces. If cats are not successful in the hunt, they sleep hungry. So that is a great driver. Cats teach their hunting skills to their children and group mates because the survival of the whole pride depends on the skills of everyone. (Lions are also cats, right?). Cats don't live in a fixed place and cover huge ranges in order to find prey. So they necessarily develop perspective. They learn to create strategies for a successful hunt. Cats know that their own survival depends on the wellbeing of the entire pride and so they care for one another.

For the Cat, the focus is self development & collaboration.

Arising out of this I have identified some key characteristics which I believe if a person develops he will become entrepreneurial in nature and will become a winner in all ways. I have described them in detail below but the way I conceptualize them is as one arising from the other in a glow of goodness. Becoming a cat is a lifelong journey of delight. For cats don't die. They turn into mist that rises from the forest at dawn.

Faith is the foundation of Courage

FAITH: Small word with big meaning. Means different things to different people. So let me define what I mean by 'Faith'. To me, faith is a dynamic process that is based on the individual's understanding of him/herself in the context of physical, intellectual, psychological and spiritual strength. That is why self awareness and emotional understanding is very important. Based on this s/he takes risk and has success which reinforces the faith. When there is a failure, if they analyze it and create a new strategy that also reinforces the faith. Otherwise, faith can be shaken sometimes with failures.

Faith is the sure knowledge that one will succeed in one's endeavor. To do all that is required and then to trust that the result will be favorable. This may sound irrational. But it is a very critical element of the combination. It is the final ingredient in the mix that produces success. Without faith you reach the end of your strength and find nothing to sustain you across the leap…the leap of faith. I like to use the words of Barbara Winters to describe faith:

"When you come to the end of the light of all that you know and are about to step off into the darkness of the unknown, faith is knowing that one of two things will happen; there will be something firm to stand on, or you will be taught how to fly."

For me faith is knowing with complete certainty that Allah will do what He promised in the Qur'an: Sura At-Talaaq: 2-3: "For the one who has consciousness of Allah (and fears His displeasure – has taqwa) Allah will extract him from all his difficulties. And will provide him from sources that he could not imagine. For the one who has faith in Allah, verily He (Allah) will become sufficient for him."

It is this faith that gives courage. The courage to take the unpopular stance. To speak the truth before the tyrant. To stand up for the oppressed. To do what needs to be done no matter how difficult. To follow your dream. It is this faith that lights the path on the long, dark road in the late reaches of the night when all about you are asleep and you are sitting wondering if the road that you have chosen to walk is really worth it or not. When human awareness and resistance to adversity is at its lowest, faith is the small, clear voice in your heart which tells you that what you are doing is right and gives you the courage to carry on.

Courage enables Risk-taking
When one operates with courage, taking risk becomes possible. Courage is not what you have before you start. It is what comes

when you take the first step. When you first stand up, your heart is fluttering, your knees are weak and your throat is dry. But as you stand up and all eyes turn to you, a cool breeze blows and you suddenly find steel inserted into your spine. You stand taller, your senses are enhanced, your eyes are bright and the voice that comes out of your throat is firm and confident. It is as if you are standing to one side listening to yourself speaking words you did not know you had in you. Explaining things that were themselves unclear to you until then. Yet when you start to speak, you find that not only do the concepts become clear but you are able to explain them with examples that take the breath of people away in that moment of "Aha!!" that comes not too often but is remembered for all time, when it does. What you had thought of as risky until then seems so easy and winning inevitable. And all that you are aware of is the excitement of it all.

Risk-taking creates Excitement

Excitement is the adrenalin flow no doubt. But more importantly it is the door that opens onto the vista of new possibilities. Of things unspoken and only dreamt of until then. Of concepts still in the shadows on the far boundary of knowledge. Of what may be, of what can become. Imagine that you have just reached the top of a steep mountain pass. It was a long hard climb, sometimes even dangerous. But you made it. And now you step into the pass towards the gap in the rock that is like a doorway.

As you enter the door, you come to the lip of the escarpment that overlooks a valley spread out below, at your feet. Undulating grassland, hints of blue suggesting a stream flowing into a lake in the far distance, clumps of thick shade trees, the distant cacophony of parakeets and other birds flying around from tree to tree eating at will. The mist rising in the early morning from the forest floor. Myriad smells, sights and sounds. A cool breeze comes up to greet you and invite you to step forward taking the first step on the path leading to what new discoveries you don't know yet. I will leave you to imagine the rest. Fill it with the images you want.

Experience the shortness of breath, the sparkling of your eyes the warmth of the early morning sun on your face, the hint of coming rain. Not the rain that spells cold and damp. But the life giving rain that the dry earth prays for and waits every day. This is the excitement that creates energy, commitment and drive, for excitement after all is also fear but which anticipates a happy ending.

Excitement drives Passion
Passion soars on the wings of excitement. When a person works with passion all the forces of nature collaborate to help him. Much can be done with little. All the numbers add up correctly. Time slows down to let him finish his task. The train comes on time. The taxi man returns to him the things that he forgot in the cab when he got off. Passion invokes passion. Others who come into contact with the person who works with passion get energized. Suddenly they start to see meaning in what they do which until then they had been doing mechanically. People who work with passionate people report an enhanced sense of satisfaction and accomplishment. They look forward to each day, to be with their leader and to do what pleases him.

I believe most firmly that one must identify what one is passionate about and develop expertise in it. Then when one does that work there is no stress for one is doing what one loves. It is but natural that if you love something and learn to do it, you will do it well. There is a clear difference between the work of someone who is merely doing a job and another who is answering a calling. For the one it is earning a living at best. For the other it is fulfillment of his life's purpose. It is answering a Covenant. Imagine a life that is led, every day of which is a joy to live. That is what being passionate bestows on you.

Passion drives Excellence
It is but natural that someone who is passionate about something will want to do it in the best possible manner. And that is what excellence is all about. To continuously search for a better way, a more profitable, compassionate, beautiful or exciting way to accomplish the goal. It is excellence which makes you do that which the world may consider strange. Excellence is to care more than others think is wise; to risk more than others think is safe; to dream more than others think is practical; and to expect from oneself more than others think is possible. It is only in the search for excellence that new discoveries are made and better ways are found. It is not competing against others but a race to achieve one's own potential by pushing the boundaries of one's own knowledge, capability, power and influence. Striving for excellence generates respect, attracts followers and enhances ones influence.

Excellence creates Brand
And in the end the result of this virtuous spiral is 'differentiation'. Why differentiate? Because differentiation creates brand. Brand creates loyalty. Loyalty creates influence and is the foundation of leadership. Brand creates identity. It enables the leader to stand out and not blend in with the crowd. It makes him the standard bearer to whose standard the others rally. It makes him the light in the darkness which those who are lost seek, to find the

wayonce again. Positive differentiation creates customers who are loyal and who choose you over your competitors. Producers of products and services strive to differentiate from their competition in ways that are desirable to their customers and which address a particular key need of their clients so that their clients will choose their product or service over that of their competitors'. The same logic applies in human development. The drive for excellence enables the person to create that positive differentiation which makes him a brand in himself.

And that is the essence of being a Cat. To be the best that you can be, without worrying about what the other is doing. You still do the best that you can do even if nobody is looking. You behave with grace, nobility, compassion, wisdom and honor not because of what others are doing or not doing but because you are YOU. You do it because your behavior defines you and it arises from your beliefs and values. You do, so you get, so you are. And that is what your legacy is.

To live the message that success is to do the best that you can do because only that, is worthy of you.

CULTURE AND THE FAMILY

"The business and family love are
two different, mutually exclusive issues.
When the two mix, both self destruct."

Culture's Consequences

Not every business starts as a 'Family Business'. Startups that are made by single entrepreneurs may go through many years before any of the family of the founders get involved. Not every business started by an individual is even necessarily entrepreneurial, in the sense of risk taking, aggressively pursuing opportunities and so on. And not every large non-family corporation is bureaucratic. Be that as it may, the complexities of the family business start the moment the founder's families start to get involved. And continue and increase with each generation. These complexities are very different in businesses run by the founding family from businesses where the founder/family is not in the driving seat (William Boeing, 1916; Henry Ford, 1903; Sony, Masaru Ibuka, Akio Morita, 1957).

In my view there are two principal questions that are at the root of the complexity and which must be clarified and dealt with to enable the business to transcend its birth pangs.

Current Existence & Growth: Who has the power and why?
Performance versus identity: Who are you versus what did you do?
Succession: Family or business: Which comes first?
Competence versus connection: Which is more important?

Families that understand these two questions and are able to address them succeed in perpetuating their growth, influence and wealth. Others disintegrate in internal strife and are relegated to the pages of PhD thesis on the subject of 'Family Business.' I have called this ability to deal with these questions, **'The Critical Transition from being Person-led to becoming Process-driven'**.

As a student of history I am very intrigued also to see the same critical transition that decides the fate of dynasties and nations. Where leaders have succeeded in enabling this transition and have created a law, a constitution and a methodology of perpetuating their civilization, their influence has endured long after they themselves disappeared.

Where the leadership was primarily person-led and the leader was larger than life, the nation declined and collapsed soon after the leader ceased to lead. The transition from being Person-led to Process-driven was never made and the nation vanished from the main stage of global and even local influence. Interestingly the same critical transition applies to socio-political causes. Where dynamic, charismatic leaders espoused causes (Gandhiji and others) but they or their organizations did not make the Critical Transition, the cause died after them and a Narendra Modi came to power in the homeland of Gandhiji himself. The same tragic story can be told about many other wonderful initiatives none of which outlasted their founders and the first generation.

On the other hand we have the initiative of micro-credit that was started by the Nobel Laureate Mohammed Yunus of Grameen Bank in Bangladesh, which thanks to being highly process driven looks all-set to outlast its founder.

Ideas always outlast their proponents and continue to influence, even those that may have been instrumental in opposing and terminating the rule of the original leaders. History shows us how usurpers and conquerors removed the leaders but adopted their ways and perpetuated their ideology as if it was their own.
Example: The idea of Oligarchy was initiated by the Romans. They invented the specific language to project the rule by the

wealthy as democracy. They invented the language and mental models which pictured everything non-Roman as barbaric, to be feared and fought against. The invented the idea that patriotism was the same as supporting the government in power and by inference opposing the government in power was actually being traitorous to the country. The Roman Empire is now gone almost 2000 years. But these ideas remain alive and well and are still practiced by those who inherited the mantle of the Romans. This clearly shows that what perpetuates is the system, the process, the conceptualized learning. Not the individual leader's charisma or charm or power. Even where individual leaders are hugely respected or even worshiped their teachings and ways, if not conceptualized and converted to replicable processes, die away once the first generation goes.

Ironically many charismatic, powerful leaders are allergic to emerging leadership and feel threatened, little realizing that it is in the development of these potential challengers that their own immortality lies. If they are able to inspire the young leaders, their legacy will outlast them. If not, it dies when they die.

Family business is more about family than about business
INDIA AND THE MIDDLE EAST

One thing that I learnt in my practice is that in the East, the family business is more about family than about business. Consequently religion, culture, social norms, family connections, marriage alliances, tradition and manners play a very big role in how the business is run. None of these things may find mention in a conventional business school course but are prime movers for all decision making in the families that eventually hire the products of the business schools. That is why in family business consulting, knowledge of the culture and religion is essential to understand the way in which decisions are made and why they are made. It is only when the consultant is culturally sensitive and knowledgeable that s/he can suggest solutions which are likely to be accepted. I have seen too many cases of Western consultants suggesting good ideas but which are not accepted because they don't fit into the cultural/religious context of the family. I have seen families take decisions which were bad for the business but which were more acceptable in the cultural context.

This is certainly true for Indian and Middle Eastern cultures but may well have elements that apply to other cultures as well. I have focused on these two cultures as I have an 'insider's view' of them and therefore the advantage of knowing extensively how these cultures work.

That gives me the benefit of perspective from which I am able to conceptualize the processes involved and help family business owners see the changes that they need to make in order to transform. It enables me to empathize with the specific cultural challenges that they face, the emotional dilemmas, the complexity of multiple roles and multiple role players. It enables me to suggest solutions to them in syntax that makes sense to them and to show them ways of accomplishing the transformation in ways that protect their particular vulnerabilities. Having grown up in these cultures and having studied the languages and theology of the religions, I am also aware of the very different interpretation of time that Eastern cultures have, compared to the West. It is not that time does not have value or that there is no sense of urgency. It is just that time has a different meaning and urgency is interpreted in terms of many different factors that impact on the way business is done in these cultures.

I will give you two examples: One is about a family business in India which is a very large infrastructure corporation that builds highways, airports, bridges and such large projects. This family also has a sugar mill in their village, which they still run though more often than not, it makes losses. When I was discussing some issues of the business with the founder he mentioned this sugar mill. My instant reaction coming out of my own very Western training and business degree was, "Why on earth do you still have that sugar mill? It just doesn't fit in with anything else in your portfolio and takes up a lot of your personal time and resources while the profits it makes are not worth taking about. Why don't you just sell it?"

He is a very gentle man. Most unlike the popular profile of the billionaire industrialist that he is. He said to me softly, "Sir, those people depend on us, you see."

I asked, "Which people?"

He said, "O! The people of our village and other villages in that area. They grow sugarcane and we are the only sugar mill in that whole area. If we close, they have nowhere to sell their produce. This business does not make us money but it is their only source of livelihood. How can I sell it?"

"But the new buyer will run it and they will have their income," I said; still thinking with my business consultant hat on.
He simply replied, "But the buyer will not be one of them, you see. I am one of them. They are mine. To the buyer it will be a business. For me this is a legacy. I have to honor it." And that closed the case.

Family is Family

There is always a difference between 'insiders' who are family members and 'outsiders' who are not related. Some of these differences may be overt as in rules applied differently. Some may be covert and under the surface but still clearly visible to everyone, as in forms of address, precedence, who can go to the Chairman's home uninvited. In many families the business is treated as an extension of the family home and the same roles of elder and younger apply.

Employees are 'servants' and in India the word 'Malik' (Owner) is used to refer to the business head. The connotation is not limited to the legal issue of business ownership but is extended to the 'Malik' being viewed as the 'Owner' of everyone who works for him. Loyalty is therefore a very personal thing and is experienced as such. Someone who is not completely in sync with the 'Malik' has really no future in the business. Being in sync is often interpreted as being subservient. This means that any difference of opinion can mean a quick termination of career in the business. For family members this is even more complex because in many cases they have literally 'nowhere to go' if they leave the family fold.

Guaranteed employment

Every male (in some families daughters also enter the business) member enters the business as a matter of course, whether there is any need for him or not. So, many don't even look elsewhere. Many don't care if they do well at school or not as they are sure of a job. Such default entries later have trouble inspiring and leading executive staff who are career driven. Such staff compare the family leaders to business leaders that they may have experienced in multinational process driven businesses and if they don't measure up positively professionals have trouble being led by them. Some play politics and decide not to rock the boat and accept the incompetent family member in order to keep their jobs. There is an overall lowering of standard of leadership in the business and profitability and growth suffers.

Guaranteed career progress and no door marked 'Exit'

Like employment, career progress is also guaranteed. After all the family rarely promotes an 'outsider' over the head of an 'insider'. So the family member will always get his promotion, even if it means that someone else actually does the work. I have seen many examples of this in the Middle East where the professional manager actually does the work while the family member is busy fulfilling decorative purposes. Needless to say the same logic extends to family members leaving the organization. After all, just as you can't steal from yourself, you also can't leave yourself. So no exits for any of the reasons that are guaranteed to send 'outsiders' into orbit. Needless to say this encourages complacency. In some families the incompetent member is shifted to some other part of the business where he proceeds to spread his negative influence, only to be moved elsewhere when he has done sufficient damage. The power of the bad apple must never be underestimated.

Hardship is what hungry Indians have to undergo

When a Western child leaves his food the mother says, "Think of all the starving Indians. Don't leave your food." As if by his eating the bellies of the starving Indians would be filled. What I am alluding to is almost all 2nd and 3rd generation family members would never have seen financial hardship. They would never have known what is means to want something but not be able to get it. For the 1st generation founder it is almost a matter of honor not to allow his family to 'suffer' what he may have suffered in the startup phase. The fact that this suffering built character, resilience, energy, self reliance and confidence is lost sight of. As a reaction to the hardship that he endured the founder tries to give the 'best' to his children. It is in the definition of 'best' that the complexity lies. Usually 'best' means easiest, most comfortable, cushiest, most expensive, and most glamorous. This only encourages decadence, self importance, false sense of security and a love of ease. For Generation 2 & 3 getting money to buy something is a simple matter of asking Daddy or if Daddy is reluctant then asking Mommy to facilitate the process which most mothers are only too happy to do. For many even that is not required because all that they really want is usually given to them on one occasion or other and for the rest there is oodles of pocket money.

The other side of the coin: The 'Burden of the Family'
Who loses his seat? Who loses his head? Who loses his job? Who loses his home? Who gets paid first? Who takes the first salary cut?

It was reported in the US once that the Ambassador of one of the Middle Eastern kingdoms was once asked why they needed to have a dictatorial rule in their land. I understand that he replied, "In your country when the government changes you lose your seat. In my country we lose our heads."

In the case of family businesses the other side of the coin is the other meaning of 'Family is after all family'. These are the people to whom the place actually belongs. So they are the ones who in the end will be left holding the can if something goes wrong. Many founders hock everything including their wife's jewelry, their homes and their reputations to raise funds. If the business fails, they stand to lose everything, while a professional who works in that company simply walks away to another job and talks about the last job as a 'learning experience'. The potential of loss to the owner is far more personal. He is the one who will pay the price personally for the risk. No matter how dedicated the employee may be he is not personally liable. Similarly if things get tough the founder is the first one to forego his salary and to take a salary cut while it is a matter of honor for him to ensure that his staff never has to do the same. Rare indeed is the staff member who <u>volunteers</u> to take a salary cut when the going gets tough. This is the single most critical factor that builds the 'insider' - 'outsider' mindset.

I have seen situations where a close friend who was with the founder at the start got an 'insider' status because of how he helped the latter in a tough situation even though he was not a family member. Some of these outsider-insiders become powerful beyond measure and wield authority even over younger family members. This becomes the cause of much heartache among the younger generation but they can do little about it as long as the sponsor of the insider-outsider is alive. It is this sense of personal commitment to the business that truly distinguishes the owner from others.

Speed is the result of power: Owner versus Employee
Play by the rules versus make new rules: Another factor in the discussion that we have been having is the power of the owner to decide things. Customers like to deal with owners because they can get decisions. The owner has the power to decide, to change rules to make new rules, and choose to do business in new ways. Most employees have to follow policy guidelines and so are

slowed down and their hands are tied in some cases. Many owners are very wary of handing over authority to other family members, let alone employees and like to make all decisions themselves. Many take pride in micromanaging oblivious to the fact that this is the biggest barrier to the growth and development of the business. They are themselves involved in all kinds of minor decisions that there is little time or inclination to think about the long term or to work on expansion or diversification. In the end of course, everything adds up and the result is not beneficial, to say the least.

Of Founders and Followers

The founder is the source of all power in the organization. There was nothing until he/she started the company. He does the gate keeping (who comes in and who does not), he pays the salaries and it is his/her vision often unarticulated but understood by a small group close to him, which is being implemented. The founder inspires his core group and takes the risks. It is his money, name and reputation on the line and the return is fame, credibility and wealth. Those that follow the founders are usually family members because they are the first ones who are available or some close friends. They follow the founder because they share the vision but also because in some ways they could not have done on their own what the founder achieved.

They recognize in his talent, their own inadequacy and that in helping the founder they are actually helping themselves.

At this stage the organization usually has a 'paper board' or a 'rubber stamp' board whose job is really only to approve what the founder/CEO has already decided. This tends to become the rule and is a cause of much distress later, when the organization grows beyond a certain size. This tends to breed a degree of hero worship and where the founder allows it, even sycophancy. In it lie the seeds of the downfall. The main factors that contribute to entrepreneurial success; risk taking, working to a strategy and inspiring others to follow his lead; are seen as the personal qualities of the founder and reach an iconic status.

Little or no effort is made to conceptualize them and attempt to teach them to anyone else. The main challenge of the founder at the startup stage is to manage working capital which means a very strong focus on production, sales and collections. The founder and all with him are 'chasing numbers'.

There is very little time or inclination for anything else even when there is an understanding of the need for long term people development. People development is paid a lot of lip service, is mentioned in every Chairman's message in every annual report and becomes the footnote in every corporate communication. But nothing more happens. No real development happens and the excuse is the same in every instance, "No time!" People development is seen more as a 'nice to have' rather than something that is critical to growth and progress. So the minute there is pressure on the cash flow the first thing that is cut is the training budget. This state of affairs can continue for a while but not for long and slowly it takes its toll.

As the founder acquires assets, the focus shifts from risk and growth to control and safety. It is truly said that the bravest man is one who has nothing to lose. Founders of successful businesses begin to acquire assets and realize that they have much to lose and so very quickly all their founding courage bleeds away and is replaced by the fear of losing assets. Very logical and reasonable, no doubt, but potentially disastrous. Rule books are written and their administrators acquire prominence over all others. 'Loyalty', 'Obedience' and 'Compliance' all become the keys to success. 'Risk', 'Independence', 'Difference of opinion', 'Questioning' all become sins. Accountants become more powerful than revenue generators. Difference of opinion, especially with the founder or his family is interpreted as 'opposition' and becomes a ticket to a career outside the organization. Similarly independence is seen as rebellion and questioning is seen as going against authority and so 'disloyal'.

Vicious spiral

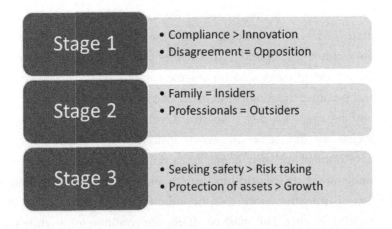

Family members acquire even more significance because they are seen as most 'loyal' and 'trustworthy' as they are 'insiders' while professionals are seen as 'outsiders' and so by inference less 'trustworthy' and 'loyal'. The organization collects obedient disciples who may well be great at implementing instructions but not much else. Mistakes are treated as failures at best and crimes at worst and are punished. Consequently, all intelligent people avoid making mistakes in the only sure way, by taking no initiative or risk.

One of the interesting things about culture in family businesses is the extent to which the personal culture of the family becomes the culture of the business. For example, in India, Africa and the Middle East (and in Indian and Middle Eastern family businesses elsewhere), the joint family culture continues to be the operative, dominant culture in most business families. In this culture hierarchies are rigidly defined, can't possibly be superseded and are a matter of birth and end with death. The patriarch is the head of the family and remains the head until his death, no matter how old or feeble he may become. He is succeeded by the eldest surviving male member of the family, either his brother or son. And this continues.

In India, according to the Hindu Personal Law the head of the family is called the 'Kartha' and is permitted to file a joint income tax return for the whole family, which is a major benefit as everyone is not taxed separately. The same cultural structures persist in Muslim families though the Income Tax Department does not recognize a Muslim Kartha for tax purposes, even though he performs the same function. Be that as it may the position of the family head is very powerful and its influence extends through the generations. In this system if you are not fortunate enough to be born early then your turn at leadership will probably never come and there is nothing that you can do about it except to break away. And that is what often happens.

Naturally this does not happen overnight. So over time a lot of resentment builds up at imposed authority that is sanctioned by society. Politics within the family also starts up with different people taking sides. Women play a very powerful behind the scenes role where they influence their men in one way or the other. Tradition and social rituals and customs add to the resentment. The family hierarchy dictates social standing and so the younger ones have to kowtow to the elders in all public ceremonies and functions no matter how much they may dislike doing it.

Boundaries of official and personal interaction are blurred. As one young man from a very prominent Indian business family said in a group once, "The Chairman to you, is Tauji (Uncle-the father's elder brother) to me. I go home with him, you don't. I have to touch his feet, you don't." What happens in the office becomes an extension of what happens in the home. Causes for resentment can be many and powerful. Loyalties are by blood relationships which sometimes get influenced by marriage. 'Scion A' marries the daughter of his uncle and then his ties with that part of the family become stronger. Not that he will be disloyal to his father but when it comes to competing with his brothers he will have the additional force of the uncle's side of the family behind him.

For an outsider (consultant) to even understand these dynamics it is almost obligatory to be an insider first. Meaning that you need to know the native language of the family and be from or have a deep understanding of the culture/religion that the family follows. The boundaries between religion and culture are also blurred and many things which actually have nothing to do with the religion but are really elements of the local culture, get the sanctity of religious rituals. And since they have been followed for centuries in cultures that have a high degree of connection with their roots, they have great influencing power.

For a Western mind it is very difficult to understand how family history and tradition that is centuries old can have any relevance at all today. But in the East history is a living thing. It may not all be factual but it is believed nevertheless and gives us a sense of identity and belonging which is highly valued and jealously guarded. Like all things there are two sides to this as well.

On the one hand Westerners are not weighed down by tradition but then they often don't have a strong sense of identity with the large extended family group. Easterners however have a very strong sense of who they are and what they stand for; things which come very much in handy especially during stressful times. They have a strong connection with their roots and family bonds are very strong. 'Family' in these cultures is not merely the nuclear relationships but a vast extended network involving marriage alliances and children of what in the West would be several separate families. All are seen as part of the clan and each has its privileges and responsibilities in a rigidly stratified system. In societies where the state does not bear the burden of social security, the family ties are critical to survival. This is recognized and respected and where necessary, enforced. People are not always free to do whatever they want because what they choose to do can jeopardize the whole system and others may suffer the consequences. So freedom is not experienced in the same way as it is in the West. Mutual responsibility is a big consideration in Eastern cultures. There is always someone to take care of you, but with this comes the burden of tradition and all its boundaries. Honor is a big part of the equation and public opinion is a living thing that influences decisions strongly. For example I have seen in several Muslim and Hindu business families (it is amazing how many traditions are similar) that as a mark of respect, the younger members of the family will not sit in the presence of the patriarch or any of his siblings, the uncles. Neither will they smoke or even speak or laugh loudly in their presence, even if the elders do, as a mark of deep respect for them. This behavior is expected, rewarded and its absence strongly objected to and even sanctioned when the young one refuses to give up his 'waywardness'. The conditioning however is so strong that I have personally never seen any instance of anyone actually defying this tradition of 'showing respect' to elders.

The question of course is not about sitting or standing but the carry forward of this tradition of showing respect into the Board room. Which son, who will not even sit in the presence of his father, would or could speak against his father's point of view, especially in the presence of others? In such a scenario what chance do you think an 'outsider' professional manager has of taking a stance opposed to the heavy weights in the family? Professional managers are also judged by the same yardstick, the degree to which they are seen as 'loyal'. In these cultures power is derived from your identity, from who you are. Not from what you have or have done. Achievement is important, but is second to the position of birth. So if an elder member is not performing to par in the business, he is almost never questioned, because of his social position. In many families a younger one is put as an understudy to him, but with the unspoken responsibility to take up the slack and see that the commercial results come. It is a very subtle system and for the most part works well as long as the market remained the way it was, with the future being an extrapolation of the past. However today, when the future is nothing like the past, this system is showing a lot of strain, if not becoming completely out of place. Consequently, the need to make the business process driven.

In one very large Indian business family it is the tradition that when the patriarch travels anywhere, one of the managers of the company that he is visiting is always in attendance, 24x7. So while he is sleeping in the bedroom in the guest house, the manager (and has to be a fairly senior one, not some pipsqueak) sits in the living room, watching TV with the volume turned down, right through the night. Every 8 hours the shift changes. Reason? 'In case He calls.' It is also the expected form that the head of the location meets the flight and formally 'receives' the visiting patriarch or uncles at the airport and sees them off, no matter what time the flight may come in or leave. His wife is expected to be in attendance likewise on the wife of the visitor if she accompanies her husband. This rule extends to the next generation also but with more junior members of the professional management taking the place of the location head.

That is why in that corporation it is an unwritten rule only to hire people from the same religious community, who are not actually related to the family but because they follow the same socio-religious cultural customs, they understand them and will know what to do and will not resent the servile overtones. On the contrary for them, to be chosen to be in attendance is actually seen as a sign of high favor and an honor and is a source of perceived power for the individual. Closeness to the seat of power devolves power upon the individual. Many professionals have reported in survey after survey that one of the principal reasons they join family organizations is for the chance to be close to the source of power. In a large multi-national this may never happen. It was not a simple punishment when in the days of old someone was banished from the 'Presence'. That was almost as good as getting a death sentence. Being banished from the presence of the seat of power meant that you no longer mattered. Not many survived that banishment.

In the Eastern tradition disagreement is often viewed as opposition and therefore by inference as disloyalty. Disloyalty in this system is a capital crime. Nothing is considered worse. And that is why those who are considered loyal are forgiven all other 'sins'. Things like contribution to the business, demonstrated entrepreneurship, ability to inspire others and take them with you, are all way down on the list of priorities. The last one is also sometimes viewed with suspicion and the individual is seen as a potential threat, especially if he or she is unwise enough to rock the boat. This is one big reason why in most Indian and Middle Eastern family businesses succession is neither planned nor successors consciously developed. Capable successors are feared.

And since there is no legitimate way to succeed the only way is to break away or overthrow the older generation. Our histories are replete with instances of dynasties where rulers lost their seats by virtue of losing their heads, literally, at the hands of their own sons and brothers. In the West where the son or daughter leaves home at 18, and where the traditions about what is respectful and what is not are almost diametrically opposite there is no sense of obligation on the parents to look after their children once they have attained maturity. For Westerners to understand a system where children are treated as children no matter what age they may be is almost impossible. I remember a conversation with an American friend who was concerned that his 18 year old daughter was still living with them. In many Eastern cultures parents would have a heart attack if their 18 year old, unmarried daughter said that she wanted to move out of their family home.

In the Eastern tradition it is the responsibility of the family (sanctioned by society) to look after its own. This applies even more to daughters whose leaving home to live on their own without some compelling reason is seen as a reflection on the family honor. A family that turns out a son or daughter because they were incompetent in business would invite social sanction and disapproval. It would blight the 'name' of the family as people who don't look after their own. From the perspective of business logic however this is anathema because keeping non-performers in the organization is detrimental to the whole. Non-performers must be ejected as the health of the organization depends on this. However in a family this is unthinkable. After all you can't just turn out a son because he does not get business results.

There is much confusion in most business families about what to do with non-contributing family members. The only way of 'taking care' of family seems to be by keeping them in the business. However negative or incompetent people have a disastrous effect on the morale of others, especially when they are themselves seen as powerful by association with the family. I am not talking about someone who misappropriates funds or does something dishonest. I am talking about someone who is not competent in business and does not produce results. If that person had been a professional, he would have been sacked without question. But if he is a family member he is usually shifted around from one job to another. All that is achieved is that his attitude spreads. The fact that the only reason he still has a job is because of his family's name on the door, is not lost on anyone. That such a situation will in the long run destroy the whole business and consequently the whole family will suffer, is something that is conveniently ignored, most often because the family has no process to confront each other constructively. Consequently family members have a different status in the business no matter what their designation may be and no matter what the official line on career progression may be. The fact remains that the family member has lifetime employment and his family is looked after, no matter whether he is productive or not. Once again social traditions outweigh good business processes with attendant consequences.

Transforming by chance or by choice?
It may seem as you read the above, that given the nature of issues with family businesses it is almost impossible for them to transform their intrinsic character and become process-driven. This is actually not so. It is eminently possible to transform and I am going to show you the way to do it but let me say at the outset that it is not an easy job. It is essential to be mentally prepared for the difficulty so that you don't quit. Some families make this transition because they have no choice since the growth is very rapid and there are not enough children to go around (RPG, Tata). So professionals are taken in and processes are created. Others transform by choice (Murugappa). The choice is ours. It means basically changing the reasons for prominence, influence and control. It means fundamentally changing the way we think and in many cases actually going against traditions that have the weight of centuries of followership. But unless this is done the transition from person-led to process-driven will never happen and the organization will never be able to unlock its potential to become a market leader.

Facing the Fears
There are two major fears that founders have to deal with if they are to successfully induct key professionals and introduce a process based approach.
1. I will lose control of how things are run

2. I will lose money because the non-family professional will not treat my money the way I do.

Let us see what needs to be done if you are to overcome these fears. To begin with I will not tell you that these fears are unrealistic. They are real and all founders have them. But if you are serious about transformation, then these fears have to be dealt with and overcome. The way to do this is detailed below:

I will lose control of how things are run

You will not 'lose' control but you will consciously and deliberately 'give up' control to some extent and this is eminently desirable. This is because firstly this is the best way to develop successors and secondly because you need to free up your time to look at bigger issues. If you are involved in daily transactional matters then the organization will suffer. When you hand over control to a professional, do remember that the incumbent has the education and experience to handle what you are giving him. You are not really taking any substantial risk because you are handing over to a capable person. Secondly you are always there to see what is going on and to help him to perform. While saying that let me pre-warn you that looking over his shoulder constantly or asking him to 'check with you' every time he moves, is not the way to do this. You as the founder have to learn to trust others. If you are interested in the growth of your business and in attracting the best talent and in leaving a legacy that endures long after you, then you have to learn to trust people.

Hire the best. Some founders hire incapable people because they come cheap, then when they fail; they try to tell themselves that delegation is not practical. The fault is not with delegation but with the way you chose the person to delegate to. So hire the best, because the cost of hiring the best will be more than justified and offset by the quality of their output. Satisfy yourself that the person is capable of the responsibility and then leave him alone to perform. Mutually set goals, agree on measurement parameters and then set in a structured appraisal system. Reward handsomely and give him a stake in his own success. Clarify what kind of reporting you need for your own peace of mind. And THEN LEAVE HIM ALONE. This is very important. Professionals who have not worked with family businesses may take a bit of time getting used to this style, but those who are interested in the responsibility and in learning to work with family businesses will make the effort.

I will lose money because the non-family professional will not treat my money the way I do
Once again in this case it is a question of trusting that the professional will treat the company's money with respect. There are two things to do in this case. One is to create a culture of openness and thrift which you reinforce by your own practice. Focus on cost effectiveness, not on cost cutting per se. Always ask and teach people to ask, "What is the return on this investment?" Collect data about cost effective management and give them visibility. Reward people for giving suggestions for cost effective ways of managing and put the suggestions into practice. When you create a culture that continuously focuses on how to make the operation more profitable, then people will not spend money unnecessarily.

The second method which must go hand in hand is effective financial control. Automate and use technology to track all expenses. Get comparative data to see what others are doing. But don't create bureaucracy. That is the biggest danger in this step. Bureaucracy slows you down and makes you less responsive to the customer. Both are lethal dangers. Good financial controls backed by automation will help you to ensure that your money is not being lost and that it is being used in the best possible way. Once again, leave the professionals to do their work and keep track of their performance through your reporting systems.

In some cases a third piece of advice has to be given. If you are so wary of delegating and handing over to a professional, then define which aspect of your business are you most worried about handing over to someone else and keep that to yourself. Hand over the rest. Then when some credibility builds, you can think of handing over that 'critical' piece as well. but delegation is an absolute MUST.

The key factor in the case of family businesses is not simply to turn around 180° but to do so while keeping the good parts of family traditions alive. Change must be brought about but with the least possible pain.

It must be remembered that in the end decisions are far more 'personal' than they are in a Western corporation. In short this means that 'family will always be family' still the business must be process-driven. That is why an in-depth knowledge and personal understanding of the social and religious traditions is such an important element of all family business consulting in the East. **Family business tends to be more about family than about business.** Decision making is not based purely on cost – benefit analysis. Many other factors play decisive roles. Keeping the family together while making any changes is by far the most important consideration of all.

We will examine below what it takes to do this: keep the family together while transforming the business to becoming process driven. Before I go into the details of that, let me state with all the emphasis at my command that if this transformation does not happen, the business will decline and eventually disappear, taking the family with it. Transforming the business is therefore also more for the sake of the family than for the business. It is in the interest of both to ensure that they give it their full support so that both the family and the business may prosper undiminished from one generation to the next.

'The business and family love are two different, mutually exclusive things. When the two mix, both self destruct.'

Of similes and families

It is interesting for me from the point of view of being a social scientist that many organizations call themselves a 'family', little realizing what a bad simile that is. Family hierarchies are rigid. Position is by birth; lasts until death without the possibility of any movement between the levels and there's a very low level of transparency. The son can never 'become' the father nor can he supersede his elder brother or uncle. Neither can he question his elders about anything they do or oppose their actions openly. So he shows his dissatisfaction in subtle ways which are visible but not blatant enough to attract sanctions. However they are in turn resented by the elders who show their displeasure in many ways. A vicious spiral that eventually can have only one ending; breakup.

Professional organizations need to be places of good collegiate relationships with a high degree of transparency, teamwork between equals, and possibility of free movement up the hierarchy depending purely on individual contribution and freedom to question, disagree and make mistakes without being penalized. All these things are contrary to traditional 'family' dynamics. I realize that what I have written may seem to be an overly critical view of things but I believe that it is in fact the single biggest impediment to making the transformation from being person-led to process-driven. A family by definition is person-led. Making the transformation is about doing everything which goes against what is stereotypically the grain of the 'family'. But this is essential to do if the family and the business are to continue to be productive and profitable from one generation to the next. It is a strange paradox that when health of the business takes precedence in decision making, it is the family which becomes stronger.

Families which realize this, support the change efforts. It is a challenge for the sponsor of any change process in the family to 'sell' this idea to the rest of the family so that people can visualize the benefits of the change. In most situations it is one key family member who sees the need for change and invites a consultant to come in. If this is the founder/family head then it is easier for all concerned. If not, there is a further complexity of selling the idea to the founder/family. I have personally been both successful and unsuccessful in this process and can say from personal experience that it is not an easy thing to do. However it must be done. The balancing act that the consultant has to do without any safety net to hold him will put the most hair raising circus tightrope act to shame. On the one hand he/she has to retain the confidence of the sponsor. On the other hand he has to win the confidence of the founder/family who may not see things in the same light. Many founders see the introduction of consultants to bring about transformational changes as a direct attack against their authority.

That fear has to be dealt with and laid to rest. While doing this it is essential not to pretend that nothing is happening because transformation is about fundamental change. What must be done is to show how the transformation will actually help the family and not simply create turmoil.

Characteristically the anxiety tends to be very high and unless the benefits of the change are clear, there is every likelihood that the anxiety will overwhelm the enthusiasm. It is essential for the consultant to be sensitive to the dynamics of the change and be very aware of the factors that may be causing the anxiety. Detailed knowledge about the family, their circumstances, knowing personally as many of the stake holders in the 'game' as possible, their traditions, religious and social issues and culture is essential. A close relationship between the consultant and the sponsor is essential but this must be as unobtrusive as possible because given the nature of what the change can mean for some people it is likely that the consultant will be seen as the 'hatchet man' of the sponsor. That is very detrimental to the whole atmosphere and does no good to the change process at all apart from being disastrous for the consultant himself.

In Eastern cultures many other factors also impact. For example, the age of the consultant. Young consultants don't stand a chance because by definition they have less experience. Older professionals have an advantage as they would have worked with many different clients and can bring all that experience to bear. Younger people tend to be seen as operating purely from a theoretical framework and so except in the more definite forms of consulting like legal, accounting and finance; they don't get into the inner circle of confidence as easily as older people. However I have myself used the benefit of the door opening for one thing to broaden the scope of my work by winning the confidence of the client, and so would like to say that if the younger person has the wisdom, facilitation skills and knowledge of the cultural context, it is possible to take on the role of family business consultant without the benefit of grey hair. The issue is of gaining acceptance of key family members.

I've already mentioned the importance of a cultural match and so will not repeat myself here, but that is a very critical element. Finally women, in the role of family business consultants, tend to have a far more difficult time than men, as there seems to some level of gender discrimination in this matter. In most Eastern business families women tend to be kept out of real business roles. So for the men to accept a woman as an advisor is very difficult. In my view both, keeping family women out of business roles as well as not accepting women consultants is completely uncalled for and a loss for business owners because given the nature of family businesses, women with their greater sensitivity and gentleness are at an advantage if given a chance. However in most families where male members are aplenty, women are relegated to running charitable foundations or educational institutions and the like and not allowed to run businesses even though many may have the education to do so. It is only when there is either no male handy or when the woman is unusually assertive and/or has the support of one of the older men that we see a woman in the board room. This worldview devolves upon the woman consultant as well and so women tend to have a harder time of making an entry into this field. Naturally this is a generalization but one which I believe is correct. Be that as it may, the barrier exists and must be surmounted.

Family versus Professional: Subjective versus Objective

Let me attempt to briefly summarize the challenges of transforming a person-led family business into a professional process-driven business. Before we do that however let me state once more in case you have forgotten that whether we like it or not, there is only one way to make a business globally competitive, attractive to the right talent that is necessary for growth and outlast its founders and endure over time; and that is to make it process-driven. But at the risk of repeating myself, **transformation by definition means total change, not incremental gradual tinkering.**

Family business versus Process Driven Business
The Dichotomies

Family Business	Process Driven Business
• Family comes first	• Company comes first
• Guaranteed employment to family; automatic entry	• Employment only to those most suitable to the position
• Family members can't be sacked	• Anybody can be sacked
• Loyalty to the family comes first and foremost	• Loyalty is primarily to self and own career, then to the company
• Power comes by birth or by being 'close' to the family	• Power comes from performance and delivery beyond expectations
• Low transparency especially in financial matters	• High transparency especially in financial matters
• Some people are beyond being questioned on	• Anyone can ask questions to anyone else

anything	about anything
• 'Who' is usually more important than 'What'	• 'What' is always more important than 'Who'
• 'Respect' is for 'Who', not 'What'	• 'Respect' is for 'What', not 'Who'
• Questioning and disagreement is seen as opposition especially if it is to family members	• Questioning and disagreement are seen as essential leadership qualities and appreciated
• Different strokes for different folks, especially family members	• One rule applies to all, especially to Top Management
• Salary, perks, privileges depend on genes (family) not jeans (work)	• Salary, perks, privileges depend on complexity of work and track record
• Career progress depends on many factors including being 'liked' by family members	• Career progress depends on only one factor, consistent performance beyond expectations
• Family members inherit positions	• Everyone has to earn their position
• Family members don't necessarily have a professional 'market value' of their own	• People are hired and paid on the basis of their current 'market value' so they all know it well
• Family members make the critical decisions, especially those about growth and investment	• People who are professionally qualified to make such decisions, make and have to justify them
• Family members lose	• Professionals lose their

their 'homes' for a bad decision • Owners manage whether they are professionally qualified or not	jobs and call it a 'learning experience' • Only those who are professionally qualified manage

The purpose of this list is not to scare you. That would be counterproductive to facilitating the change that I believe family businesses need to make. I made this list so that we understand both the magnitude and the criticality of the issues we face when we set upon the road to transform the business and make it process driven. Also so that we realize fully the benefits that will accrue if we choose to take the steps that may be difficult sometimes and sometimes even painful.

Only when our vision is firmly set upon the gain from the goal does it become possible to bear the difficulty of the path.

By no means are all family organizations as 'bad' as I have described but I have seen too many of them on this road to believe that I am wrong. I believe that breaking up in the 3rd or 4th generation is not only possible but almost inevitable unless the critical transition from person-led to process-driven is made. However in many cases the current situation is that there is money to burn and the family does not realize or deliberately ignores the potential dangers in the future because it is more convenient to do so, rather than to take action to save the situation. Especially when such action will mean taking some hard decisions. I can't think of a single case where an individual or an organization succeeded because it <u>could not or would not</u> take hard decisions.

One must realize that it is not merely the survival of an organization that is a hallmark of its success. Survival is a boundary condition. Not an achievement. It is growth, a global name and presence, impact on the environment, service to society and contribution to learning that define world class organizations. GE for example is known more for creating global business leaders than for its various products or financial turnover or ROI to the shareholder. These are the natural outcomes of the kind of people it nurtures and produces. The people are its real contribution to society and thereby to its own growth and eminence. There are many family businesses which are the same age as GE and had the same opportunities to grow and impact their environment. But not one of them (still run by the founding family directly) is even in the same league. This for me merely underlines my contention that as long as the critical transition is not made the family business will never break through its self-imposed barrier to growth and significance.

The Making of an Entrepreneur

So what is it that differentiates an entrepreneur from others? Being an entrepreneur myself (A full member of the 'Honorable Society of the Educated Unemployable' since 1994) I have thought much on this subject. I want to share my thoughts with you, the reader. These are by no means rules or pronouncements but working thoughts in my own attempt at understanding entrepreneurship. It is my belief that if one can inculcate entrepreneurship in people then one can inspire them to take charge of their lives and do great things. Entrepreneurship is by no means restricted to founding businesses. It is a quality that anyone can develop and practice anywhere. It has to do with an approach to life that is different.

Entrepreneurship: Love for business

"Entrepreneurs are entrepreneurs because they are entrepreneurial in nature and by preference."

Now that may sound like an oxymoron but I believe that entrepreneurs, meaning specifically people who go into business, take risk, make deals and so on, are inclined that way by their nature itself. Entrepreneurship is an essential part of all good organizational cultures. While entrepreneurship can be taught I do believe that a lot of it is intrinsic to the individual. Training brings it out more and inculcates awareness for it in those who may not be so inclined.

But entrepreneurship as we know it in business; making deals, taking risk, seeing opportunity where others only see difficulty; is a matter of a person's nature. This may be the result of inborn character or childhood conditioning but some people are predisposed to doing business. That is what I am led to believe having closely interacted with many highly successful entrepreneurs and being one myself, as well as having read numerous case histories of people who started business ventures. There is a particular streak in their nature which makes them 'unemployable' by others.

It gives them a nose for a good deal and makes them willing to take risk and trust hunches. Now, not all business is about hunches or unsubstantiated risk, but there does come a time where prudent people back off but the hard core entrepreneur will go ahead and win the situation. Within organizations also entrepreneurial people tend to take decisions, often without asking for 'permission' for things which they feel confident about. They tend to regularly step out of their box of defined authority to get the job done. They tend to make commitments which they expect the organization to support, being more conscious of losing customers than of 'offending' superiors. Unfortunately in many organizations, notwithstanding all the lip service paid to the need for employees to take 'ownership, accountability and be entrepreneurial in nature' when someone actually behaves with a sense of ownership to the business, he or she usually gets a sharp rap on the wrist for their efforts from insecure egotistic bosses. Most entrepreneurial people can't take much of such treatment and so they leave.

That is why I would like to start with that trait or element of nature that founders of business have. There is no evidence to prove that this is a genetically transmitted quality and so it is not necessary that a businessman's son or daughter is ideally suited for or inclined towards business. Dirubhai Ambani's (Reliance) father was no businessman and neither was Narayana Murthy's

(Infosys). However both started two of the most successful billion dollar businesses in India. I do believe however that the 'legends of the household' do play a part in conditioning a child's mind towards business. Just as these legends predispose children towards a career in the military or academics or social service. That is why perhaps in India the image of 'business communities' has been formed. In the Middle East it is people from Yemen (Hadramauth) who are considered to be astute in business. Most of the major business families in Saudi Arabia for example are from this region. Naturally the child born in a Marwari or Chettiar or Hadrami home is more likely to hear stories of deals and business wins than a child born in a Jat Sikh, Pathan or Moghal family. Those children will hear stories of war, valor, brave deeds and hardship borne for the sake of the nation. That is what I was brought up on as I was growing up. But then I became a businessman. So who said life was simple, eh!!

So there is the effect of conditioning which drives one towards making money. I have no statistically valid data to prove any of this; just personal experience and anecdotal information. Be that as it may I do believe that the primary reason why people do business is because they want to do business. They may have other alternatives but they choose to do business. It is this inner nature also which sustains them through difficulties and failures. People with the inner urge to do business never even consider anything else. If one business fails they start another. But they never consider not doing business and applying for a job in some company or the other. Those who opt out of business are the ones who did not have this urge in the first place but decided to go into business as many young professionals today seem to want to do because of some foggy notions of the 'glamour' of being a business owner. They forget the hard work and sacrifice that come in the same package and jump in with unrealistic expectations.

Then at the first failure, they give up and run back to the corporate world and tell stories about how difficult it is to succeed in business in this country or that. All the while the businessman quietly continues with his work, his mind alive with ideas, seeking more and without even the thought that he could possibly be doing anything else. In my view therefore the foundation of any business is this spirit of entrepreneurship, the desire to participate in commerce, to buy, to sell and to build an organization that does all this.

I remember calling on Mr. A.M.M. Arunachalam, the head of the Murugappa Family and the former Chairman of the Murugappa Group after he had retired. I was in Chennai on some work and it was my custom always to call on him and pay my respects, so I telephoned and his secretary asked me to come to the office.

I was surprised as I thought having retired; he would have been at home. When I met him, I asked him, "Sir, I thought you had retired and that you would be relaxing at home." He said to me, "Yawar, what do you think I am doing here? I am relaxing. Business is relaxation for me. This is what I love and this is what keeps me healthy."

So the first quality is entrepreneurship. A love for doing business. The freedom of being your own person. The discipline to hold yourself to a tougher schedule than any employer would have put you on. The process, the excitement, the risk, the sacrifices, the long hours. The desire to inspire others to work with you and 'invest' in you; time, energy, money, ideas. The willingness to put your resources on the line and to work to make that a success. A love for the feeling of winning when you make it a success. That is the first quality.

'Choosing' a business or 'Lucky accident?'

"You learn to do business in the same way as you learn to ride a horse or a bicycle, by falling down many times, but getting back in saddle every time you fall. Business is a contact sport."

Most business founders that I have spoken to, have said that they did not start off into business after doing any detailed market research or analysis to see which would be the most profitable line of business to be in. Neither did they have a clear idea of being in the particular line that they eventually became big or famous in. They just started doing business, all the while being open to new ideas. Then some opportunity would come up and they would go into that. Eventually, some after several 'deviations' would settle on something that they really liked to do and was profitable. That became their 'main business'. What helped them was that they knew how to do business.

How to raise funds, make a profit and build an organization. The actual content or nature of the business was immaterial. What was material is that it was a good profit making opportunity and they knew how to use it. **All the deviations were really training in how to do business.**

Case in Point

Dhirubhai Ambani started as a gas station attendant, went on to become an executive in that company and could have gone up in the organization if he had stayed with them. But he didn't. He returned from Aden to Bombay and became a yarn trader. Why yarn? Because that looked like a good business. It could have been something else just as easily. What did he know about yarn trading? Nothing to begin with and everything very quickly thereafter. Someone asked him how he learnt. He said, "I listen to people and I read. And I know how to get from here to there and I do it." Then came the opportunity to go into petrochemicals and he did.

The result? What the Tatas took 100 years to do, Ambani did double that in 40 years. And yarn? That is less than 2% of the business today.

http://en.wikipedia.org/wiki/Dhirubhai_Ambani#_note-18. The Wikipedia link has a lot more information but I believe my point is made. Entrepreneurs are not passionate about any particular product or service, they are passionate about business. They try many things, keep what works and drop what flops. And they are learning all the time. They don't start off with deep studies. They just start to do business because that is how you learn it. They listen to people but they make their own decisions. They are open to feedback, have little or no ego and are willing to change, themselves or their track. Remember, this desire to learn may not even be conscious. But it happens. And over time they settle into their 'line' and become known in it.

This is by no means to imply that there is anything wrong about a good detailed study of the environment before going into business. It is just to acknowledge that in the end it is not the result of the study but the inner urge to do business that drives the entrepreneur. If the study had shown that this particular idea would not fly, they would not give up the idea of doing business. They would simply find another idea. Or maybe, they do what the bumblebee does; fly anyway. They start, they make mistakes, they learn, they change their ways, products services, attitudes. What they never change is the idea of doing business. As they say, the laws of aerodynamics show that bumblebees can't fly. But bumblebees don't know aerodynamics. So they fly.

Two important qualities in this that one needs to remember:
1. The willingness to own responsibility for one's decisions and derive learnings from them
2. The willingness to be open to change

Everything is changeable except the idea of doing business. Moving from one business to another is a simple matter, but while one is in that business, one puts in their maximum physical and emotional energy into it. I don't know of any successful business founders who did anything half heartedly. Passion is everything. If one can't get emotional about what one does, then perhaps one is in the wrong business.

There is only one way to win and that is to give it all you have. Nobody understands this better than an entrepreneur. Those who don't, fail.

Willingness to learn from mistakes
I can't possibly emphasize the importance of creating an atmosphere where people are free to learn from mistakes. We all know that success depends on good judgment; good judgment comes with experience and experience comes from bad judgment. But in order for bad judgment to result in good experience some other things must happen first. The first requirement is a clear differentiation between a 'mistake' and a 'crime'. It begins with the intention.

A crime is something that is premeditated or at least the result of refusal to exercise due care despite having the knowhow and awareness. This naturally attracts punishment in some form or other. A mistake on the other hand is a wrong judgment despite the best of intentions often as a result of taking risk with the intention of achieving remarkable results. In the course of this attempt perhaps some critical factor was missed and so some loss happens.

The two, crime and mistake, can't be treated equally. If you do that you will kill all risk taking and entrepreneurship as happens in far too many organizations. The interesting fact is that in our languages we don't seem to have a word for a 'good try that did not succeed'. But it is only when people take the risk of failure that they push the boundaries of the known to make the impossible, possible. To learn from mistakes first requires a mindset change. From treating mistakes as failures or crimes to realizing that mistakes are really good intentioned, sincere efforts that just didn't make it.

I suggest the following method to inculcate a culture of learning.

From: 'Mistake = failure' to 'Mistake = learning opportunity'

1. **Accept responsibility for your actions:** Don't blame anyone else. Own up that it was your fault.
2. **Examine/analyze what went wrong:** See what you did or could have done.
3. **Fix it and share your learning with others:** Ensure that it can never happen again.
4. **Monitor it:** Put in a system to ensure that your fix is working.

If you follow this system you will progressively make the entire system fool proof and in the bargain engender an attitude of trust, openness and continuous learning. Give it a try and you will see it for yourself.

Entrepreneurs make mistakes. Sometimes deliberately. What I mean by that is, that they will do things that they are very unsure about simply to see what the reaction from the environment is.
How else can you know about the reaction of the customer unless you are prepared to face the customer? So they do. Sometimes the reactions are not what they would have liked to see. They are not discouraged.

They go back to the 'drawing board' – often in their own minds – and redesign their approach. Then they go back to the customer. Entrepreneurs are not afraid of criticism. They have the discrimination to sift the valuable from the trash. They are not bogged down by comments which are really jealousy and other negative emotions masquerading as constructive criticism. They don't engage with the people who make those comments. They don't respond to those comments. In short they don't gather trash. They gather value. They listen to those who are really interested in seeing them succeed, even though what they have to say may sound harsh. They appreciate the intention behind the words and listen carefully without trying to justify their own stances. Then they make changes in what they do. The most exciting thing about being an entrepreneur for me is the constant learning. Nothing beats the thrill of that. To take risk and win.

Inspiring followership

"How big a leader you are depends on how many followers you have. How many people believe in you and that depends on how many people you benefit. Leadership is about what you contribute. Not about what you consume."

Successful entrepreneurs have the ability to enable others to dream their dream. They are able to translate their vision into something that others find meaning in and are able to see how they can fulfill their own dreams through it. It is true that not everyone who follows the founder is the ideal person that the founder needs. But then it is equally true that most founders are strapped for cash and so can't really pay for top talent and so have to make do with whoever is willing to do whatever needs to be done. However they have the key skill to make something out of nothing. They don't complain. They identify the best in people and use it. They ignore what is not useful or negative. And lo and behold, people who others had given up on, flower in the company of the true entrepreneur and become productive and creative. It is all in the approach, attitude and treatment. You treat people as if they are already what they can be and they become what they have the potential to become. I have seen this again and again in my own life.

I know one highly successful entrepreneur who started in business going with his friend on the back of his scooter to sell software door to door. Another whose friend used to bring him lunch which his wife had cooked for both of them. A third whose friend and business partner continued to work in a regular job and supported his friend from his salary, while the friend hit the road building their business. After 2 years the friend managed to get Intel to put money into the business as venture capital at which time they both went into the business full time. All these and many similar stories relate to how entrepreneurs are able to inspire others to invest in their dreams.

People who have been with entrepreneurs at the startup phase have a huge emotional investment in their leader. The tell stories about how the leader in return invested time, money and energy in helping his followers. I have heard stories of how one entrepreneur sat in the hospital all night keeping vigil while his friend's child was sick and the friend was away on an assignment. Another one who used to coach his partner's children in physics for their exam. A third who would call the entire startup team, home every Saturday and cook fish for them himself, which they all loved. It was not so much with doing earth shaking things. It was more the whole issue of investing personal time and energy in subordinates and colleagues. This wins the hearts of people and energizes them to outdo each other to help the entrepreneur to succeed. Successful entrepreneurs always pay their debts. That is one universal fact that I have never seen change anywhere. It inspires loyalty and love. But in the long run, this sometimes becomes the single biggest stumbling block to making the business process driven. Most entrepreneurs are unwilling to compromise on this and let their faithful startup companions go, simply because they no longer fit into the now much bigger and more complex business. They suffer the inconvenience of having to carry someone who is not pulling his weight any longer than the dishonor of being unfaithful to a friend who had helped them when there was nobody else willing to have faith in them.

This sense of honor is a very important, often unstated, ingredient in the decision making of Eastern entrepreneurs. I have suggested to some to put their faithful friends on special offline projects in areas like real estate development or facilities administration or overseeing travel and that seems to work well. The friend has something meaningful that he can handle and the entrepreneur has an honorable way to get him out of the mainstream where he was a hurdle for others. It is a combination of these three qualities that makes the successful entrepreneur.

Successors must perpetuate success

"In the end it is your legacy that defines you. That legacy will play itself out when you can do nothing to influence it. Yet its win is your win and its failure also yours. What happens then will not be a factor of what you could do then, but of what you did or failed to do, long before the team entered the field. Businesses as matches are won or lost in the mind first."

I have always wondered what you would call successors who don't succeed. It is like the question, "What do you call a lift (elevator) going down?" Successors are intended to succeed. All founders can be assumed to have that objective for obvious reasons. But successors all too often fail. The lift continues not to lift but to go down. The business declines, the family breaks up in acrimonious courtroom or boardroom battles and history is repeated once more.

Intensions are the basis of action but not all intensions are converted to actions. And without action, results don't happen. Founders do intend to have capable successors, but in most families succession planning is almost never done systematically. It becomes something that just happens because the founder dies or is otherwise unable to participate in the business any more. Successors are often unprepared and incapable with predictable results. Succession planning is about anticipating the only definite thing in the life cycle of the business, which is that one day you will no longer be there. It is about enhancing the 'bench strength' of the company. It is about creating not one but multiple players who can play in your spot so that the team never suffers from a loss of expertise.

There are three steps to succession planning:
1. Identifying the 'right' candidates
2. Systematic training & mentoring
3. Objectively assessing results

Identifying the 'right' candidates
Needless to say, identifying the right candidate is essential. For this one must 'spread the net' wide. Identify the key competencies and attitudes that you are looking for and then take into account all those who fit. This must be done on the basis of an objective 360 degree appraisal so that those who don't make it in the first cut are clear what they need to do to make the mark.

I will not go into the details of designing and implementing the 360 degree appraisal exercise as that is outside the scope of this book and will suffice to say that it is a commonly followed method in world business leaders like GE, Motorola, Toyota and others. The earlier this exercise is done, preferably while the first generation is still in the seat, the better. Competencies and attitudes necessary for leadership must be designed and described specific to the organization though some may be generic in nature. Their operative definitions must definitely be organization specific. So it is not simply a matter of listing some common virtues. The exercise takes time but is a one-time effort and well worth whatever it takes. Once it is completed and everyone is clear about what it takes to succeed in your organization one can start the next step. It is essential to make this a public exercise as any kind of secrecy is detrimental and breeds rumor and misunderstanding.

Systematic training & mentoring

The next step is to prepare those who have the capability as well as to narrow the field somewhat. I have suggested a top management structure (Executive Council) that will simplify the selection of successors. Training potential successors is a long term and high contact matter. It requires a combination of three strategies:

Working Opportunities

Projects of graduated difficulty in which the incumbent/s can show their capability. These are also good opportunities for them to build working relationships with key professionals in the organization. Some of these projects may even be outside the organization or may be of a troubleshooting nature. It is essential to ensure that projects of sufficient variety are given both to train the individuals in different skill areas as well as to identify any special talents or interests.

Assessment & New Assignments

Work on the projects must be assessed regularly and sufficient assistance given to ensure success. The objective is not to catch them doing wrong but to ensure that they do right. Assessment must be on mutually pre-agreed parameters and by a process of first peer rating followed by assessment by the Executive Council. This is an excellent method also to create bonds between family members and professionals and build relationships of collegiate respect. Key strengths and wins must be identified, celebrated and leveraged. Key weaknesses/losses must be discussed, solutions sought and their development monitored. Objectivity and measurement are the keys to success in this exercise.

Mentoring

Finally I have already suggested mentoring as a tool for successor development, in the last chapter but will mention it here once again as it is a part of the whole program. Good mentoring is a result of connecting capable seniors to juniors with potential so that both can benefit. Mentors must be selected on the basis of their own personal track record as well as their inclination and ability to teach others. Some of them may have special expertise which can be leveraged and several juniors apprenticed to them to learn that particular skill. Mentors in family businesses need not all be family members. Many family businesses select capable professionals to mentor young scions of the family. This is a mutually beneficial exercise because to be selected to mentor high potential youngsters is a matter of pride for the one selected. This also enables future leaders to form relationships of mutual respect with key professionals by working with them at a different level. It acknowledges the supremacy and importance of learning and the position of the teacher as being worthy of respect no matter what his position may be in the company hierarchy.

Objectively assessing results

Finally at the end of the training period, results must be evaluated and decisions taken about how the potential successor has fared and what more needs to be done. As we have seen above results are being assessed all along as the projects and mentoring progresses. Here I am referring to the annual as well as the end-of-program assessment based on which decisions will need to be taken. Once again I recommend peer rating followed by rating by the Executive Council which will ensure a high degree of transparency and objectivity in the process. To maintain the credibility of the process both are absolutely critical. Measurement parameters would already have been set at the beginning of the program as mentioned above. Assessment will be based on them with the incumbent having an opportunity at the end of the assessment to address the Executive Council. That will be the formal 'graduation', after which the incumbent will be in the official list of potential successors.

In conclusion it must be remembered that enhancing the bench strength of the company is the most important task of the top management and CEO. That is the family's guarantee to successfully handing over the business from one generation to the next. As they say in the army, 'It takes 40 years to make a General.' So also in business, world class leaders are not created overnight and definitely not by giving them fancy designations. What is essential is that the individual develops real bandwidth in terms of expertise, experience, social skills, negotiating ability, political/influencing knack and patience. All this takes time, thoughtful intervention, structured opportunity and above all, the willingness to learn.

ENDURING LEADERSHIP™

ORGANIZATIONAL EXCELLENCE MODEL

"It is a strange paradox; to build a great organization, you have to shift your focus from what benefits the family to what benefits all your constituents. But funnily when you do that, it is you and your family who benefit the most."

Diagnosing your Current State

To understand what is happening in a family business and to diagnose its state of wellbeing it is essential to look for signs of the transition (Person to Process) which I have mentioned earlier. So how does one know if this transition is happening or not? And what must one do to make it happen and avoid the possibility of the negative vicious spiral? Let me start by giving you a diagnostic tool to assess if you need to make this transformation in your business. I call it my diagnostic tool as it will help you to diagnose if your business has terminal illness.

Family Business Terminal Illness – Diagnostic Tool

Please answer the following 7 questions: Remember it is your business.

1. Do owners also follow rules?
2. What matters more: 'What was done?' or 'Who did it?'
3. Do you reward those who disagree with you?
4. Do people earn or inherit positions?
5. Do position holders have a market value of their own?
6. Who makes the key investment decisions? Family or non-family?
7. What happens if the professional boss of a young family member has reason to terminate his employment?

For each of the above questions you should be able to support your answer with hard data.

Answers: Indicating terminal illness

Do owners also follow rules?

No. Our rule is different strokes for different folks. Family members are above organizational policy. After all we own the bloody place, for God's sake. We make the rules. So why do we have to follow them?

What matters more: 'What was done?' or 'Who did it?'
When what was done is equal, 'who' tips the scale. After all a family member is a family member, see?

Do you reward those who disagree with you?
Reward for disagreeing? Are you crazy?

Do people earn or inherit positions?
Performance Appraisal Interview:
Boss, "You joined this company as a Manager, two years ago. The following year you became a General Manager and now we are planning to make you a Director."
Subordinate, "Thanks Dad!"

Do position holders have a market value of their own?
Can I get a job at the level I am at here, in Wal-Mart, Unilever, P&G or GE? Sure! When my daddy buys that company. Hahahahaha!!!

Who makes the key investment decisions? Family or non-family?
Well, it is our money, right? So how can anyone else make investment decisions?

What happens if the professional boss of a young family member has reason to terminate his employment?
You are joking, right?

Bottom Line

In the final analysis the issue is very simple. Which comes first; the family or the business? If the former comes first both will perish. If the latter gets precedence, then both with flourish. The choice is open. But it can mean some hard decisions.

The Realities
(Something that does not change whether you believe it or not)

Do owners also follow rules?
If those who make the rules don't follow them, it sabotages the authority of the rule like nothing else. Owners must exemplify obedience to the rules in every respect.

What matters more: 'What was done?' or 'Who did it?'
There is nothing more demoralizing for professionals than to see the glass ceiling defined by genetic accident. There is nothing which builds more credibility and trust than fair, results-based assessment across the board.

Do you reward those who disagree with you?
This must be done visibly and regularly. The disagreement must be recorded. The individual who disagrees must be asked to come up with an alternative which must be considered seriously. Where it is not adopted the reasons must be explained satisfactorily to the individual.

Do people earn or inherit positions?
The surest sign of this is to examine the basis of promotions. All promotions must be based on competence, experience and demonstrated results. No exceptions to the rule.

Do position holders have a market value of their own?

If the incumbent in the role (family member or professional) applied for a job at the same level in a global MNC competitor organization, would they be considered? Family businesses hire professionals from global MNCs because of their experience and the systems that they feel they can bring to their company. Such professionals have a benchmark against which they will measure the family members. The degree of respect they feel (not show!) for family members will depend on how they measure up against the global business leaders that these professionals have experienced in the companies they worked for before they joined the family business. Leaders add value to their followers. What value do you add?

Who makes the key investment decisions? Family or non-family?

Because it is your money it makes the greatest sense to put it in the hands of those who have the experience and knowledge to invest it to get the best returns. These may well be family members themselves who have made the effort to get the education and experience necessary. But where this is not so, professionals who have such experience must take precedence. And this must happen because the family's future prosperity is at stake.

What happens if the professional boss of a young family member has reason to terminate his employment?

What happens if the same professional boss has reason to terminate the service of another young professional? The same must happen here as well. If not, you just sabotaged yourself. This is easy to do if you only remember that this happens in Wal-Mart, P&G, Unilever, Merck, Sony and many others; all of whom started as family businesses.

Success is about making choices. And all choices have consequences.

The Critical Mindset Change

The most critical mindset on which this entire transformation is based is:

The family needs the business and depends on it, so the business comes first. The business depends on customers, so they come first. Employees work for the business, not for the family. As a shareholder your wealth will increase only if the business does well. If you insert incompetent children into the business just because nobody else will hire them or because that is a way to avoid tax on what you pay them, then you are cutting your own throat.

All entrants into the business, irrespective of what their surname is, must demonstrate their eligibility to enter, stay and grow. **The business and family love are two different, mutually exclusive issues. When the two mix, both self destruct.** This mindset is the precondition to all that I am about to suggest. Unless this mindset is established as an inalienable rule, no change will last or be beneficial. I want to make this absolutely clear to the reader.

Here I would like to emphasize once again that for any family that is interested in the business outlasting the founders and continuing to support the family through multiple generations, transforming from being person-led to process-driven is not a matter of choice. It is essential to survival itself. Even more so to growth, development and perpetuation over time. In the following pages I have suggested two models for this transformation: one at the organizational level and another at the individual level and finally some suggestions that are specific to business families and their members. I trust you, the reader, will find them useful.

4 - Basic Assumptions

I am making 4 – basic assumptions about the individual and the organization:
1. The individual desires to be a part of an organization to fulfill certain personal needs, both material and psychological
2. The organization desires the membership of the individual to fulfill its own goals which it can only do using the talents of the individual
3. That while these two objectives are not mutually exclusive, they will also not automatically mesh without conscious effort
4. That if eventually organizational and individual goals are to be realized, then this meshing or alignment is absolutely critical

Challenges for the Entrepreneur

The main challenge for the entrepreneur is to translate his/her vision into an actual action plan for the organization. This comprises of three stages:

1. Enabling others to dream your dream
2. Translate the dream into a concrete structures which will ensure desirable behavior
3. Reinforce the behavior with training, measurement, monitoring and reward systems.

In my experience many entrepreneurs are inspirational by temperament and nature and rely on this personal inspiration to do the trick of energizing others. This works for a while when the organization is small and the leadership style can afford to be personal. However, their very success creates the challenge of still conveying the inspiration when it is no longer possible to be in personal touch with every employee. Many entrepreneurs are not big on setting up systems to ensure that the original inspiration is transferred 'automatically' and so eventually it remains dependent on the energy of one individual or his core group. This is a recipe for eventual failure as the success of the organization and its size become its biggest blocks. The key to success in my view is in actually reducing 'inspiration' to a measurable and implementable commodity.

To illustrate, a good example of this translation of traditionally 'non-measurable' values into implementable parameters is the development of the Lexus, where design engineers asked the owners of luxury cars like Rolls Royce, Mercedes, Jaguar and Bentley, apparently 'vague' and 'non-definitive' questions like, "What do you feel when you sit behind the steering wheel?"; "What do you feel when you sit in the back seat with your chauffer driving?"; "What do you feel when you shut the door and hear a solid 'thump'?"

They then proceeded to translate these emotion and feeling level answers into engineering drawings which resulted in the production of the fastest selling luxury car in the world. Translating vision into actionable parameters is precisely this: translating emotional responses into actionable items which can be seen, measured and reinforced. Without this rigor of 'translating', the vision remains a dream and is never realized to its full potential.

Moving from being Person-Led to being Process-Driven
The key challenge to growth of entrepreneurial organizations is this transition from being person led or driven to becoming process driven. It can safely be said that this is such a critical threshold that it can spell the difference between success and phenomenal growth or eventual failure. As I mentioned earlier, it is the causal loop of the success of the entrepreneur that sets up the compensating loop of the challenges of growth. Any entrepreneur who has energy and access to funds will be able to build a large organization fairly quickly. However the skills that he or she needs to make the large organization succeed are very different and in many ways almost the opposite of what made him or her succeed in the first place. Consequently many entrepreneurs fail to make the transition and yet another dream does not come true.

Just to give you an idea of the almost diametric difference in skills and attitude between being a start-up entrepreneur and the leader of a large global company, I have listed randomly some that come immediately to mind. I am sure you can add to this list from your own experience.

New skills need to be learnt but unfortunately most entrepreneurs when they reach a stage of eminence and are the heads of large organizations consider themselves as having 'arrived', especially when it comes to interpersonal skills. If you are in this category and don't agree, then please see how many interpersonal skills development programs you attended in last 12 months. And if you are planning to tell me that you did not have the time, I rest my case. It is at this time that external advisors or a family business consultant can do the most good. Unfortunately many business owners are very reluctant to take advice except from those who they know will agree with them and shun those who make them uncomfortable by asking difficult questions.

Leadership Skills in a Start up	Leadership Skills in a Global Business
1. Willingness to get your 'hands dirty'	1. Willing to delegate
2. Leading from the front	2. Leading from the 'rear' by developing others
3. Being able to do every job personally	3. Setting up systems for everyone
4. Being 'everywhere for everyone'	4. Allowing others to take decisions without consulting you
5. Being all things to all people	5. Letting others become significant

Many organizations articulate a "Vision Statement" or a "Mission Statement" usually because ISO or some other quality certification requires that they have such statements, but that is where it often ends. There is neither real understanding of the power of the structure nor any belief that this clarity can actually do them good in a business sense. These statements show up in corporate brochures and on the walls of the Chairman's office. However if you were to stop one of the employees and ask him/her what the vision of the organization was, not one would be able to tell you what it was. I had this experience once with a senior HR manager who told me, "We did an exercise to arrive at our core values. There are some 6 or 7. I can't remember them all but I think one of them is entrepreneurship." I kept a straight face and asked him, "How did you define entrepreneurship?" He looked totally blankly at me and had no idea what I meant by 'defining entrepreneurship'. But the reality is that without clear definitions of what the value will look like in practice; one can never measure it or be sure that it is actually being practiced. Values that are not practiced are mere words which do nothing to help the organization in any way whatsoever. In fact they do more harm than good because they destroy credibility.

Credibility falls through the gap between Stated and Practiced Values.

My Enduring Leadership™ model has two critical foci. One aimed at the organization as a whole and the other at the people in the organization, at all levels, who go to make the organization great. Each reinforces the other to ensure that all energy is leveraged.

Pride in Identity

I first want to deal with the word 'pride' and differentiate it from arrogance. This is very important because if pride exceeds its boundary and becomes arrogance, then it is no longer a positive force but a strongly negative one. In my definition taking 'Pride' in the organization is to have a strong sense of confidence, love for, desire to be identified by and defined as a member of the organization.

The basis of my model of Enduring Leadership™ is a strong sense of identity that is well understood in all its detail such that it invokes a strong sense of pride and belonging. A good way to understand this is the regimental identity that a person in the military has. The regiment gives him or her, a sense of who they are, what it means to belong to this particular regiment and how this is different from belonging to any other regiment. What the regimental values are, what the uniform and accoutrements are, what the colors are and what they mean. What the regimental song is, what its battle cry is and so on. All of these things serve to emphasize the 'benefit' of belonging to this regiment and the individual derives a sense of pride from being a member of this regiment.

Many things reinforce this sense of identity. Rituals, like special ways of greeting, chants, songs, meeting methods especially starts and finishes, clothing, medals, hats, ties crests and logos; are all the paraphernalia of branding. People who 'belong' are conscious of what this means, what the organization stands for, what its members can or are not expected to do. They are knowledgeable about their history, especially about incidents of having overcome difficulties and are proud of it and take moral sustenance from it. They feel togetherness with others who 'belong' and follow the unwritten rule; 'Thou shalt always vote in favor of thy brother.'

The Free Masons for example are an organization that has existed from medieval times for more than 2000 years. It has a worldwide network of members who belong to local Lodges and all subscribe to the ideology of Free Masonry. Their history invokes in them a sense of pride and their rituals and legends reinforce it. People feel proud to belong and are conscious of this status. 'Old Boy Networks' are still strong and work powerfully.

I am deliberately giving you examples that are outside the corporate world for two reasons. One because the Enduring Leadership™ model is content independent. It applies to any organization, irrespective of its nuts and bolts activity. Secondly because I want to emphasize the importance of some things that commercial organizations tend to forget when it comes to building a sense of belonging in their people. It is important to remember that belonging is an emotional stance. And so it needs emotional causes and reinforcements. Throwing money at people not only does not serve the purpose but is actually counterproductive. When things are defined purely in monetary terms, they tend to be viewed in a very mercenary way and no sense of loyalty accrues. A mercenary army that fights for money is never as dedicated or passionate as an army of citizens fighting to defend their homeland. The former has no sense of belonging or mission, their stakes are not particularly high and their fight is only for the loot that they can get. For the latter it is a matter of defending their homes, children and way of life. There is no comparison between the dedication of one and the other.

Reinforcing the Identity
The foundation of Enduring Leadership™ therefore is a strong sense of identity and belonging to the organization of which their members feel proud. So what is the way to achieve this? There are two tools to develop a strong sense of identity in people.
1. Invoke Traditions that celebrate Signature Qualities
2. Reinforce alignment with exclusive Signature Structures & Rituals

Invoke Traditions that celebrate Signature Qualities

Creating tradition by Story Telling
Traditions are the tools that invoke the emotional power of the history of a people. So also in organizations. Traditions are reinforced by their stories. These stories need not be grand, of countries won and lands conquered. Simple incidents that illustrate what belonging to the organization means. People need to hear about other people. Wal-Mart people hear the story of how a young associate was running with a tray of cup cakes

which he had to get to a location in a hurry, coming around a corner he ran smack into Sam Walton. He and cakes flew in all directions. Sam simply helped him to pick up all the cakes and sent him on his way with a pat on the back saying, "Well done son, but take it easy."

Or another one about the opening of a new store. It was the tradition in Wal-Mart that when a store was ready to be opened, on the night before the opening, the team that worked on the store opening would be treated to a barbeque by Sam Walton and his Board Members. One assistant writes about the store that they were all working to set up, that the work finished at 2.00 am. As they were all washing up, what do they see? Sam and his Board members driving up. The cars came to a halt, Sam and his team got out, pulled out the makings of a barbeque and they served dinner to the entire store set-up team at 2.00 am. This is the stuff of legends and this is how traditions are celebrated. Small stories that speak volumes about what belonging to Wal-Mart means.

Or the story of Sony and how the Walkman idea came to Masaru Ibuka. He bought a Phillips Dictaphone to record a meeting when he was in Switzerland. That evening he went to a night club and recorded a song that he particularly liked on his Dictaphone. On the way back home to Japan, he listened to the song on the plane. And from that was born the idea of one of the most successful products the world has ever seen. But more importantly this story underlines the importance of entrepreneurship; of keeping an eye open for business ideas in every situation. Because as they say, Phillips still makes Dictaphones.

Or my own story when I was a young Assistant Manager and crashed my bike and badly injured my knee. I was in hospital recovering from some very painful knee surgery and had just come out of the ICU into a private room, when Mrs. M.A. Alagappan, the wife of our MD, came to visit. She enquired about my condition and then asked how the hospital food was. Then she smiled and said, "Hospital food is never good, so I have brought some fresh idlys for you." I was very touched that here was the wife of the Managing Director who had gone to all this trouble to make me comfortable when I was ill. But that was not the end of that. Every day morning and evening, her driver would bring such delicious, fresh home cooked food for me that I almost regretted leaving the hospital. Now that is what working for the Murugappa family means. Almost anyone who has worked for this family would have some such story to tell and would resonate with my feelings about the sense of belonging that we all felt.

So it is not the magnitude of what is done, but that it is done and that it is mentioned with honor. These stories are the legends of the organization and serve the same purpose as the mythology of a religion does. It adds color, it sheds light and it illustrates what it means to belong. History is preserved through stories in a very powerful emotional way that evokes energy and serves as an adhesive between people. It is important however to make this a conscious process of collection, preservation and dissemination. If stories are left to the individuals to whom they happen, they will not spread in the whole organization. They will remain isolated and more than likely leave with the individual when he or she leaves the organization.

Induction of new members is a good story telling time. But that is by no means the only time it should be done. Every opportunity must be used, for the glue that sticks people together is never enough. It needs frequent replenishment. Stories encourage other people to behave in the ways that the stories illustrate and so the tradition perpetuates.

Reinforce alignment through Structures & Rituals

Structures & Rituals to ensure that people are aligned
The purpose of the stories is to underline certain qualities that are considered desirable above all else in the organization. 3M stands for innovation, Motorola for technological excellence, GE for leadership development, Wal-Mart and Nordstrom for always serving the customer.

To reinforce these qualities 3M has the 15% and the 40% rule. Motorola has the ritual where the CEO sometimes leaves the management meeting when the discussion on technology is over and the discussion on finance starts. P&G has brands competing against one another (a marketing taboo of the highest order) to underline the importance of competition. GE spends more than $2 billion annually on its corporate university at Crotonville. Sam Walton invented the Wal-Mart chant and would end every store visit by leading the chant himself.

The purpose of all these rituals and structures is the same; to reinforce the qualities that the organization wants people to inculcate and align to in order to create a sense of belonging with pride. Each of these rituals makes the practitioner stand out. Uninitiated customers at Wal-Mart are sometimes taken unawares by the chant and I am sure it appears rather weird to many. Imagine stopping all work suddenly and all the people in the store yelling the chant together!! But for those who do it, it is a great binder and sets them apart as an exclusive group and constantly reinforces their sense of identity and belonging.

Creating rituals and structures also accomplishes another very important purpose; that of measuring alignment. Mikel Harry of 6 Sigma fame said, "If you want to know what an organization values see what they measure." I say that you can only guarantee what you can control; and you can only control what you can measure. Rituals and structures give you a measurement stick to see the degree to which people are aligned to the organization. Belief and emotion is in the heart and is not visible. Behavior is visible. Rituals and structures convert belief into behavior. Beliefs drive behavior and behavior drives results. That is why it is important to ensure that there are structures and rituals to celebrate signature qualities that you would like people to align to so that they stand out and are differentiated in the market.

The Covenant
From a strong sense of belonging with pride arises what I call 'The Covenant'. I use this term because what differentiates ordinary work from inspiring work is a sense of purpose that comes with an understanding of how it fits into the larger scheme of things. When people understand this, they realize the real value of what they are doing, no matter how insignificant, even menial, their own small job may appear to be.

The best illustration of this is the famous story of the three stone masons who were breaking stones by a construction site. A passerby asked each of them, as passersby are wont to do instead of simply passing by; what he was doing. The first replied, "I am breaking stones." The second said, "I am shaping building blocks." The third looked up and smiled. "I am building a cathedral", he said. The difference between the workers lay not in their work but in their minds. For one it was a menial job which earned him a living. Having spent his required time at it, almost as a punishment, he would then go and do whatever it was he really wanted to do.

Since the earning helped to achieve that, he was doing this job. How many are there in our organizations who come to work only because it is a job and earns them a living? And who say, "Thank God it is Friday," every weekend because they see the weekend as the reason why they patiently suffered the week.

But for the one building the cathedral the work was the reason for his existence. It was his legacy; it gave him meaning, significance and pleasure. He was after all building a cathedral which would last long after he was gone. His work, whatever its magnitude or complexity, was critical. Without it the cathedral could not be built. Each stone was important because on it would rest the massive mass of the wall.

Each stone was important because it would be one of these which would be chosen by the master mason to be the keystone in the whole edifice. Each stone was not a stone; it was a building block to something that was far more magnificent, beautiful, significant and eternal than the shaper of the stone. And through his work the shaper would also live, long after his material existence had ended. It is this sense of purpose that I call the Covenant.

I recall an incident where a business founder friend who had recently returned from the US to India and set up an IT company invited me on one Friday evening to a program he called TGIF. I asked him what TGIF meant. He said, "That God its Friday." I said to him, "Are you telling me that this is what your employees are actually saying to themselves every Friday evening? What do they say on Monday morning?" He was shocked and said to me, "I never thought of it like that! It's just something we do in the US and I thought it is a good thing to introduce here." I said to him that ideally one should aim to create a workplace where the employee says, "TGIM!!"

The Covenant is a promise. A promise that a person makes to himself, to do the best that he can. To work to fulfill his potential, to realize the purpose of his creation, to live his dreams and to become all that he can possibly become. And to do all that through his work in the organization. This Covenant arises from and is linked to the Pride in Identity that we spoke of earlier. When the pride in identity is strong, the covenant glows with its energy. One can only feel commitment to something that one feels proud of doing. One can't feel committed to something that one is ashamed of or indifferent about. So a strong sense of pride in the identity that the organization confers is essential to a strong commitment to the covenant that the person voluntarily accepts.
Voluntarism is an essential part of the Covenant. A covenant has to be accepted. It can't be thrust on the unwilling. Covenants are aspirational. Their aura makes them intensely desirable and people seek to be among those who have sworn to fulfill the covenants. Commitment is a natural outcome in people who are fulfilling a covenant. They don't need motivational speeches or incentives. The covenant is the motivation in itself and its fulfillment the best incentive. It is essential therefore to clearly put the covenant before people so that they can choose.

The Unchangeable and the Changing
In the Enduring Leadership™ model, Identity and Covenant are the two existential realities. They are eternal and are the link between one generation and the next. Each generation hands the

torch of the Covenant to the next and in the process leaves behind their own stories of struggle, triumphs and resilience to add to the repertoire of detail that will enable the new generation to see meaning in their work. For more than a century GE has homegrown leaders and given them to American industry. 3M has innovated product after product. The Tatas have built enterprises while keeping ethical values intact, sacrificing some speed of growth in the process perhaps but content in the knowledge that they have not violated their covenant with destiny. These are the unchanging.

And the changeable? The primary of those is a strategic focus.

Strategic Focus
A strategic focus is the spearhead of the Enduring Leadership™ model. It is its cutting edge. It is what enables the dream to be fulfilled. It gives context to the effort and places things in perspective. A strategic focus makes it possible for people to draw an overall plan of action before they get too closely involved in the details. A strategic focus enables scenario planning so that decision makers can foresee the possible consequences of their decisions, their potential impact and to make changes to achieve the best results. Without a strategic focus decision makers get trapped in what I call the 'Activity Trap'. This is a very common situation where people get so involved in immediate transactional activity that they lose sight of the reason why they are doing what they are doing. The activity and being busy become ends in themselves and give a false sense of achievement. But in the end when the counting is done the doer realizes that he has achieved nothing of any significance. Huge amounts of time, resources, energy and enthusiasm would have been expended, all to no real avail.

Starting with a strategic focus saves one from this most undesirable end. Decision makers work with an overall master plan. One that is not cast in concrete but which is significant enough to be taken seriously. For this reason, a clear strategic focus pre-supposes two things:

1. Good data collection and digestion
2. Good conceptualization and planning

Remember the Strategic Focus is about focus. Not about any particular strategy in itself. It is about the discipline of asking good questions about the sources, objectivity and reliability of data. Of asking, "So what is this information telling us?"

It is to use tools like scenario planning to develop alternate strategies in case circumstances change. A strategic focus is to understand that information alone is not knowledge, no matter how complex. That knowledge is not power because power comes from the way knowledge is used which we call wisdom. To remember that all action as well as choosing not to act, have consequences and these must be thought of before commencing the action. And above all, to do all of this in as short a time as possible with a sense of urgency so that the potential benefits of the action are not bled away by the delay in taking the first step.

A Strategic Focus is essential also because it empowers the other two criteria of the Enduring Leadership™ model which we will talk about below. Without a strategic focus many people tend to take short cuts with quality and deliver shoddy goods and services in order to make a quick buck but in the process they sacrifice ongoing long term gains. They deal with their constituents in short sighted ways which leaves them feeling used and abused and destroys commitment and dedication. But when we start with a clear strategic focus we understand why we do what we do and so we do it with a sense of purpose and direction that gives us leverage and enables much to be done with little.

To have a Strategic Focus on anything it is essential to first have perspective. Perspective is a function of distance. You have to mentally step back from the immediate reality and look at the big picture. Often this is very difficult to do because the immediate reality is very pressing. However if your nose is in the picture, you can never see it in its entirety. And the result is shortsighted action focused on getting symptomatic relief at the expense of long term misery. Perspective is the ability to simultaneously hold two pictures in your mind: Where you are and where you wish to be. In business process terms this means a clear awareness of the current status and a clear vision of what the 'achieved state' will be like. When organizations and leaders work from this state of mind, they are energized by the vision of the achieved state. They hold themselves accountable for all actions in terms of how they contribute to implementing the vision.

When they begin with the end in view, they don't waste time on inessentials. They are able to prioritize, focus on issues that give leverage and use their resources wisely. They see the need to develop people to perpetuate their vision. They act with the long term in view while still focusing clearly on what needs to be done immediately.

A Strategic Focus is not one versus the other. It is to understand how one meshes with the other and influences its achievement. Organizations that have institutionalized a Strategic Focus into their thinking always ask questions about how their short term policies, actions and initiatives help in achieving the long term results. They leverage the short term to achieve the long term. Choices become clearer and easy because they are defined with the big picture in mind. When you have perspective resulting in a strategic focus you can then draw a roadmap to get from where you are now to where you want to be. You can put milestones on the roadmap and plan how long it is likely to take to achieve the goal. You can plan your resources and the inputs you will need to achieve your goal. As mentioned earlier you can also plan alternate strategies in case your first one does not work out. Many things are possible provided you take a strategic approach.

Focus on Quality
The Organizational Excellence aspect of the Enduring Leadership™ model focuses on quality as the driver of all effort. I passionately believe that quality is the only guarantee of long term success. It is true that cutting corners and shoddy delivery can bring about momentary success in an undifferentiating market, but even then it has a negative effect on the memory of the customer which translates into customers going to competition at the first possible opportunity when they have a choice. So quality is key. Excellent organizations focus on quality not because it is profitable to do so or because it is expedient, but because quality is a reflection of how they see themselves. Of who they are. They work and deliver to the highest quality standards not to win any prizes but because for them, to work in any other way is inconceivable.

The Bombay Dabbawallahs are a case in point. Today they are a 6 Sigma case study. But they worked in their 6 Sigma way long before 6 Sigma became a quality standard that the corporate world even started speaking of. And certainly long before they themselves had even heard of this standard. Given the size of their organization, its composition, membership and its highly decentralized makeup I would not be surprised if one could find among them those who have no idea what 6 Sigma is, even today. However that does not prevent them from delivering hot meals to their customers with less than 3.4 mistakes per million. And that too when their 'producers' are individual housewives preparing meals for their working families and their 'delivery channel' is the Mumbai public transport. I believe can they do it, because they can't conceive of doing anything less. Quality can never happen unless it becomes a 'religion'; a matter of deep and passionate belief which people practice in their daily lives as a matter of fact. No matter whether anyone is watching or not.

Quality is also a matter of clear processes with measurements. It is not so important which quality standard one follows, though my own preference is for 6 Sigma as it measures mistakes and so correction of faults is intrinsic to it. However no matter the quality standard, the essential thing is that the standard must be believed in and practiced at all levels of the organization. It has become fashionable for some people to talk of quality standards like flavors of the month. They talk disparagingly about some 'old' quality method and in favor of some shiny new one or the other. At the time of this writing it is Lean Manufacturing as detailed in the Toyota Way which such people are talking about as if it was they who invented it. The issue in my view is not which standard one uses but how sincerely it is used. The Toyota Way works because Toyota uses it sincerely everywhere. The same is true of any other quality standard. By all means choose the one that seems most appropriate to your activity but focus on using it sincerely and not as just something to show others or present in seminars.

In India, in the late 80's there were umpteen cases of organizations declaring that they were following TQM (Total Quality Management) as a quality standard. Then some time later, you would find that nothing had really changed in their product or service delivery, their employee or customer satisfaction or in their cost efficiency. I remember the case of a steel manufacturing company that had adopted TQM with much fanfare and whose managers would produce immaculate flowcharts and tables at the monthly TQM meeting with the consultant but had done nothing to change anything in the way they actually worked. The result was that 2 years later, the company actually shut shop as they became completely unprofitable. It is surprising how such an obvious fact; that it is only in the implementation that success lies; is lost sight of so easily and people act as if simply saying that 'quality is supreme' is some kind of magic mantra which will bring about superior quality. Superior quality is the result of superior effort according to measured processes and because of a belief in being the best. It does not happen. It is made.

There are no shortcuts. And poor quality is not an option for anyone who wants to remain in business, much less for those who want to grow and prosper.

Focus on People
Developing people is not an option in building Enduring Leadership™. It is critical to success. Organizational heads who are serious about creating an organization that will endure long after they are gone treat the development of people like they treat dealing with financial assets, for example. They invest in them, they keep track of their investment, they periodically assess their

investment and they make any required changes. The Corporate Audit Staff in GE is a good example of how people with high potential are given specially selected opportunities to learn and prove themselves. Remember that this is not favoritism in any way except to allow the high potential individual to demonstrate his or her potential in action. Most of GE leaders are people who spent time on Corporate Audit. But also, the Corporate Audit has the highest record of people leaving the organization as they could not take the pressure or failed the test.

Another system that speaks of a culture of people development is the GE airplane interview. This has to do with the final selection of the CEO when the present incumbent is due to retire. The CEO selection process itself is a case study in succession planning and too lengthy to mention here. However I will suffice to say that the process consists of numerous iterations to narrow down the hopefuls to a final list of 3-4. Each of them is then taken on a flight with the current CEO in the corporate jet. When they are at cruising altitude, the current CEO asks the incumbent, "If this plane crashes and both of us die, who is ready to take over as Chairman?" The incumbent is expected to give a name immediately. When the plane lands, GE does a complete assessment of the individual named. Now comes the test of a great company: if the individual is found unfit for the Chairman's position, the incumbent who named him is facilitated to pursue his career outside GE.

I sometimes begin my Family Business seminars by asking the founders and top management this series of questions:
1. If you had to retire today who is ready to take your place?
2. How many people in your top management will agree with your choice?

3. What will happen to you if you are unable to name your successor?

Find me an organization where the CEO will be sacked on the spot if he can't name a successor and I will show you an organization that is destined to last from generation to generation. In such an organization, developing successors will be second nature at all levels. Everyone will do it. Everyone will benefit. All the time.

I don't know of any organization that prospered because it could not or would not take the hard calls. Being soft and sentimental about family members is the surest way to ensure that you demotivate everyone else and set your organization firmly on the path to self destruction. Not to take the hard calls is to be like someone who will not agree to be operated upon to remove a malignant tumor because he is afraid of the momentary pain. It is for you to decide which is more important; bearing the momentary pain or sure death. In this case, dealing with the feelings of the non-performer and his immediate family or the good of the whole family and the organization.

The biggest reason for taking the soft but fatal option is because families have no formal exit plan or criteria for their members who are not making the mark in the business. Added to this, many families have no conflict resolution process or structure in place. This is a lethal combination. I have suggested some structures later in this book to deal with such issues. Remember that these are not everyday issues. But nonetheless they are crucial to survival and instrumental is breakups. It is simply because they are not 'in-your-face' daily that we tend to ignore them and postpone dealing with them until suddenly one day we are faced with a family member who must be asked to leave. However since no preparation has been made for this, the decision is simply put aside and the family member is transferred to some other part of the business. If the reason for his non-performance is a skill or inclination based matter then this may well be a good way to deal with the matter. Some people, who don't do well in one activity, do very well in another one which captures their imagination or for which they have the necessary skills. But if it is a matter of attitude (which more often than not, it is) then it simply means that you have now transferred the 'sickness' to another part of your business to enable more people to be infected.

I was speaking at a seminar titled after this book, "The Business of Family Business", when one founder grandfather introduced me to his grandson and said, "He says, that he does not have to work hard because I have already done the hard work and set up the business. Please talk to him about this." I did not have the time to talk to him there, but thought to myself that here is someone that the grandfather must certainly not choose as his successor. The question of course is also what if any effort was made to train the successor. The answer is most likely, "None at all!"

If the desire to make a mark of your own does not exist, then how can one inculcate it in the reluctant heart? Ambition must be born. Skills to achieve it can be taught. But if one is simply focused on spending what one's elders have earned and saved, then one is a parasite. It is good to remember that there is no amount of money that can't be spent and the spenders or their dependents reduced to penury. History is replete with examples of wastrels who spent enormous fortunes and then walked the street begging bowl in hand. That is the appropriate end for such people.

Naturally this means that you as the family business head must have the skills to help people to see which path to take as well as have alternate strategies to implement to deal with non-performers. I am aware that you can't just sling them out of the front door into the street. In this book I have suggested some structures that you can implement which will help you to deal with these issues. Here it is sufficient to ask yourself if you are convinced about the need to take these hard and painful decisions. This is the burden of leadership and as a leader you need to be prepared to shoulder this burden with joy.

Imagine what such a culture does to the whole issue of people development and succession planning in the organization. In companies like GE succession planning is not something you do if you are so inclined. It is intrinsic to your own growth in the company. It is a matter of your own survival. Find me a company where the CEO will lose his job if he or she has not developed a capable subordinate, and I will show you a company which is destined to endure long after the founders are gone.

Nordstrom stores are another good example. In Nordstrom they hire only at one level. The bottom. No matter what your qualification or education, if you want to work at Nordstrom you start at the bottom. The 3 brothers who founded Nordstrom also started at the bottom, "sitting on a footstool before the customer trying on shoes". In Nordstrom they say that symbolically they maintain this position all their lives. It is not for nothing that succession is not a mystery in Nordstrom. The pathway to growth is clear. The milestones are clear and there are innumerable role models to look up to for those who aspire to lead.

Organizations that are focused on building Enduring Leadership™ are clear that the only constant is their people. Everything else can and will change. But if you have excellent people who are focused on quality, then no matter how the business changes, they will still deliver products and services that the market values which is the only formula for success. So people development is an investment item on the balance sheet and is treated as such. People are hired with the Covenant of the organization as a hiring screen over and above their technical qualifications. Development of people is systematized to dovetail with the Covenant. Reward and recognition is given for adherence to the Covenant combined with delivering above target. (As I say, 'You get a salary for meeting goals. Not awards. Awards are always for exceeding targets.').

Promotions are on merit, determined by the same two criteria: sync with Covenant and exceeding targets. And most importantly all this is continuously reinforced in actual practice. Organizations focused on creating Enduring Leadership™ never, ever act differently from their stated principles. They are too aware of how quickly credibility can be destroyed by not walking the talk. So role models of what it takes to be successful are in plenty and visible. I have discussed people development in much greater detail later in this book when we look at the Individual Development aspect of the Enduring Leadership™ model.

Implementing the Enduring Leadership™ Model
In my view the implementation of the Enduring Leadership™ model in the organization is a 3 – step process. I would like to illustrate it in the form of 3 intersecting circles.

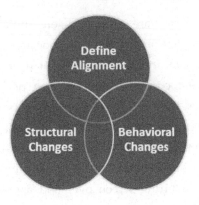

Circle 1

Articulating the identity and Covenant

This is a collective effort of the Core Group of Founders; or in the case of large existing corporations which want to implement this model it is the Core Group of Top Management. The interesting thing about this model is that it can be implemented at any stage though of course the earlier it is done the more the synergy. This group sits together and articulates the Identity Statement and then emanating from it, the Covenant for which the organization exists. Typically this exercise takes the best part of two days. There is a lot of dialogue identifying which values are core and which are not. People then work on the Operative Definitions of each value and define what it means in actual practice and what it does not mean. Then they articulate the Covenant. The pace is intense, the discussion sometimes heated. But as a result the team is welded into one. This is the fringe benefit of this exercise, to weld the family into one unit of comrades focused to creating a legacy that does them proud.

Articulating the Core Values

The Identity is based on the Core Values that the founders of the organizations hold dear. These must be clearly articulated and defined in terms of what they mean to the members of the organization as well as how they will manifest themselves visibly. For it is only when the values are practiced that their power will become visible.

A Core Value is defined as something that you will do even if you are penalized for doing it.

It is not something that is merely convenient or socially desirable or politically correct to do and for which society at large will support and reward you. It is something that you would do even if it became socially unwise to practice and may result in some kind of 'punishment' if you live by it. An example would be the value of speaking the truth in today's New World Order. Speaking the truth would be the Core Value of someone who would still do it even if he/she is punished for doing it. For all others, it may well be a value but not necessarily 'Core'. Therefore this is an exercise in self discovery and not, invention. Core Values are what we have and what we bring to the table. Not what we think we should have or which we create during this exercise because they sound good to us. Nor are they the Core Values of corporations or people we admire. Discovery, not adoption, invention or creation: is the key.

In an organizational context, this stage consists of getting individuals to dialogue about their own core values and help each other understand them. The focus is on what is, not on what 'should' be. This is the crux of this exercise without the rigor of which it quickly degenerates into wishful thinking about what 'should' happen. There are no 'right' set of core values for an organization. The 'right' set is that which generates energy for the core group. If it does not come from the heart, then it is not a core value. Usually this stage is the most difficult of the entire affair as people struggle to come to terms with each other's differences and with what they are coming together to do. Needless to say this is the first and most critical stage which requires a high standard of facilitation skill to evoke, articulate, conceptualize and gain agreement on the Core Values of the Group.

It is common to see a high level of conflict between members mainly on account of difference in understanding of what a particular Core Value means to different people. This is entirely healthy, must be encouraged but managed skillfully. A high level of facilitation skill is required to achieve this and the help of an external facilitator is an absolute must. The Family Business Consultant is the best person to drive this initiative as he would already have a relationship with the family and a position of high trust and acceptability with all the key players in the exercise.

Values in Operation: Creating 'Operative Definitions'

> *"If you want to know what an organization values, see what it measures."* ~ Mikel Harry on 6 Sigma

Once the Core Values have been identified and articulated, we go to the next step which is to create **'Operative Definitions'** for each Core Value. I developed this technique because the fact is that the energy of the Core Values can only be invoked if they are being lived by. To be able to say if a value is in operation or not we need to be able to define the behavior that reflects that value. In order to ensure ongoing synergy we need to be able to measure that behavior. Without this observation and measurement, it is impossible to say if a particular value is being lived or not. This is particularly damaging because as I have said earlier, credibility falls through the gap between stated values and practiced values. Values must be practiced and consistently so in ways that are clearly visible and measurable. That is why creating an Operative Definition for each value is so important.

The **'Operative Definition'** of each value therefore defines both <u>what it is</u> and <u>what it is not.</u> This step is very important because we can't see belief but we can see behavior. And more importantly we can measure behavior and ensure that it confirms to the standard that we set.

Two questions must be answered for each of the values:
1. What are the specific behaviors for each value that indicate that it is being practiced?
2. What are the behaviors, which will warn you that the value is not being practiced?

Operative Definitions are not only useful in resolving differences in understanding but also during the alignment stage they are invaluable in developing implementation strategies. Without good Operative Definitions, the Core Values remain philosophical statements or terms with little practical value. This stage is critical as it is this which will help or hinder the implementation process. All implementation strategy is based on the value of these definitions. And so sometimes this can take a long time.

In one case, working with a large IT software development company, on the bank of the Kaveri River in South India, living in tents, I remember that I finally went to bed at 3.00 am leaving the participants still engaged in intense debate about the Operative Definition of 'Integrity'.

The debate finished as the new dawn broke: symbolically also on the birth of their Identity. Without good Operative Definitions it is impossible to monitor implementation to ensure that the values are actually being practiced. This becomes even more important because most values tend to be expressed in words of a generic nature. For example, 'Integrity', 'Truth' or 'Customer Service' are often seen as Core Values. However unless these are specifically defined in terms of what they mean for your particular organization and its people; i.e. what the people will and will not do when exhibiting integrity, being truthful or giving good customer service, you will not be able to track if these values are actually being practiced or not. And if they are not practiced, then their benefit will not accrue.

This example from one large family business illustrates the rigor which characterizes good Operative Definitions.

What it is	What it is not
• Honesty is taking responsibility for own mistakes	• Blaming others when it is your fault
• Speaking the truth even when it may hurt you	• Manipulating the truth to suit you
• Giving just weight & measure in all of one's dealings; material or otherwise	• Not being just in business dealings • Favoritism/nepotism is unfair

• Treat all family members equally as 'your own' • Be just in all disputes	• Taking sides • Being hypocritical and having a hidden agenda

A similar operative definition must be developed for each Core Value. These definitions are written into the performance assessment forms and are measured and reported. People who exhibit these characters are rewarded and their performance is made public and they become the champions of the value. Those who don't pay attention or worse still go against the value get one chance. If they don't measure up they are dismissed. No exceptions. It is only when this rigor is applied that people will begin to see the power of the values.

Articulating the Covenant

The method I use to enable clients to articulate their covenant is to get them to think about their work and ask themselves three questions:

1. **What is it about our work that we believe is essential for our market?**
   What needs are we fulfilling? Who are we serving and how?

2. **What is it about our work that we feel proud about?**
   What is it that we are doing which nobody else can do better than we can?

3. **What would happen if we no longer did this work?**
   What would be lost for our constituents?

Then I ask them to verify their answers by looking for real hard data. This is only to reassure themselves that they are not victims of their imagination and that indeed they are doing something that is of value to their environment. When people get this reaffirming data it is a hugely energizing experience for them. They immediately start to see value in their work and any grievances and irritants which otherwise may have seemed painful are put in the right perspective; things to be dealt with but nothing to become despondent or discouraged about.

Then we ask the final question: So how would you describe what you do? Out of this exercise arises the Covenant. **A simple statement that invokes emotion and generates energy.** A statement that is easy to remember, easy on the tongue and something that people are proud to announce to the world, to be recognized for and be accountable to.

My own and the Covenant of my organization, Yawar Baig & Associates is: **'Changing the World, One Mind at a time.'** In all our work we hold ourselves accountable to this. We ask ourselves, 'How did this intervention change the minds of people? How many people did it touch? What change do we believe we have brought about? What would have happened if we had never touched the lives of these people? What will happen now? What is our way to monitor this change and to be available to them for any help that they may need? We constantly take feedback from our clients. We ask them and they tell us. We realize the importance of communicating with our customers and we do it all the time. This is of enormous benefit to us and helps us to build relationships that are not merely business focused but personally rewarding.

The Covenant, as I have described previously is in the nature of an ideology and is something that is closer to religious / ideological belief and faith than it is to any other human emotion. It is an overarching goal that is 'good for all time'. Arising out of this will come the long and short term goals. The long term goals may be in the nature of a 'vision'. And the short term goals in the nature of critical objectives for the period. The Covenant is an existential kind of belief and like all such, has enormous power to evoke energy to strive towards a goal that is seen as bigger than any personal objective of the individuals. This serves to create an adhesive that enables people to overcome personal differences and to strive together to fulfill the organization's goal.

Organizations focused on building Enduring Leadership™ are very strongly, even 'rabidly' committed to their Covenant, which may or may not make sense to the outside world. But this is unimportant. All that matters is whether it inspires its own believers to heroic effort. For it is only then that it will have served its purpose.

In the different organizations that I have worked with helping to develop Enduring Leadership™; an FMCG company defined its Covenant to be; 'Taking our products to every Indian.' The resultant energy catapulted it from the stage of another also-ran competitor to India's prime FMCG company to becoming its primary competitor.

In one NGO (illustrates how this model works independently of the nature of business) the participants described their Covenant as; 'Being the conscience of society by recording and presenting the nature of discrimination.' There is no 'right' or 'wrong' Covenant for the purpose of invoking energy, though my personal preference is for Covenants that have the general good at heart. However any Covenant is effective in invoking the energy of the system as long as it is strongly believed in and practiced, reinforced in every action and becomes the touchstone of every major decision.

Once the Identity and Covenant have been articulated, the group must identify processes in the organization that need to be aligned to them. It is a common sight in many organizations to see processes that are at cross purposes with the Covenant with predictably disastrous results. If a process is not designed to enable people to implement the Covenant, it will not get implemented. Even more problematically the process will sabotage all efforts to align to the Covenant.

For example if teamwork is a requirement to fulfill the Covenant, then the compensation and reward parameters must support teamwork and penalize individual success at the expense of others. However in many organizations the opposite happens. Then people try to correct the lack of teamwork by running teambuilding courses. All to no avail, because in fact the compensation penalizes teamwork and supports internal competition.

Similarly if customer service is an issue which you try to deal with by introducing supervisors to overlook the work of frontline staff instead of training frontline staff to become more customer oriented, you will have created more bureaucracy and slowed down the whole system, which the lack of customer focus will more than likely still remain as it was. Customer service is an attitude which must be inculcated and must drive from within. It is not achieved by having supervisors looking over people's shoulders. It is not a structural fault but a behavioral issue that must be addressed by hiring and training. Trying to correct it by excessive supervision not only does not help but creates anxiety and negatively impacts customer service which is what you are trying to improve in the first place. So correct diagnosis and correct treatment is essential for successful alignment.

It is important to prescribe the 'right medicine', as it were; Structural or Behavioral (Training). Each addresses a different need and cures a different ill. It is essential to prescribe the right intervention so that we get the desired result. The wrong intervention will not only not work but will destroy credibility in the whole process and make future changes even more difficult to implement because people would have lost faith in the change process itself. In effect both structural and behavioral interventions must support each other. The structure must make the behavior possible and facilitate it and reward it. The behavior must follow the structure and use it as a support and a source of strength and never circumvent it. If innovation is the behavior required then compensation structures, time share programs, material resources, access to knowledge bases and teachers must all be supportive of people desiring to experiment, invent and be creative. I've given other examples above.

Circle 2
Structural Changes to create alignment

Once the Identity & Covenant are articulated the next step is to look at what structural changes may be needed to create alignment of all business and people systems and processes to implement the ideology. It is in the nature of structures to influence behavior. Both physical as well as psychological structures influence what people who are in them, will do. Just as boisterous, noisy school children will spontaneously lower their voices to a whisper when they enter a library or place of worship, so also organizational structures influence the behavior of the people who work in them.

In one pharmaceutical company there was some difficulty in getting the Finance and R&D people to cooperate and work together. So we created a structure: a cross functional Council that met every week where the finance people would argue the R&D case and the R&D people would argue the finance case. We used the tool of active listening to facilitate this and it worked like magic. People started seeing life from each other's perspective and started cooperating to achieve common goals.

In another IT Services company which had a history of inter-departmental conflict and shifting of blame, we instituted a steering committee focused on business development that had among its members people from finance and human resources departments. This resulted in a change in the perspective of these traditional support staff that became proactive and energetic in actually helping the marketing and business development people to achieve their goals instead of being the proverbial millstones round their collective necks. In another one, we formally changed the designation of the head of finance from 'Financial Controller' to 'Business Facilitator'. In less than one month we could see the change in attitude of the incumbent. It may sound strange and you may think of the individual as being foolish in that a mere change in designation could make him work differently.

However as a behavioral scientist I know the power of the name. A name defines focus, identity and responsibility and changes the factors that are critical to success. For example, the factors critical to success of a Financial Controller are those that relate to ensuring that finance is controlled, meaning that people are allowed to spend as little as possible, by questioning all expenses with regard to their volume, not necessarily with respect to their impact or result. The critical success factors of the Business Facilitator are diametrically opposite. He is more concerned with the impact of the spending. Not how much was spent but how much new business came as a result. Not to say that he would allow unlimited spending. He wouldn't. But no matter how much was spent he would always ask the question, "So what is the return on this?" The change in attitude of the individual was not surprising at all. The man was merely reacting to the new role that he had been given.

Structural changes to me are like the irrigation ditches that a farmer digs to direct rain water to the plants and fields that he wants to irrigate. Without these the benefit of rain will be lost as it will not be directed to the place where it is needed the most. Without this alignment you will have systems that are in conflict with the Covenant and this will create great disruption and a loss of credibility within and outside the organization.

For example if a hospital's Covenant is to provide the best patient care possible, but it gives department heads profit related targets, then it is more than likely that patients will be prescribed unnecessary tests and investigations which will add to the hospital's earning per patient but don't necessarily add any value to the quality of care for the patient. So as far as the patient is concerned, the hospital is giving them the most expensive care, not the best care. The structure (profit targets) is not only not working towards living the Covenant (best possible care for the patient) but it is actually working against it (unnecessary, expensive investigations).

In my experience of having worked with several organizations enabling them to articulate their Identity & Covenant and getting aligned to it, it is this stage that is the game changer and in most organizations and the one that is most susceptible to going wrong.

There are two main reasons for this:
Firstly alignment usually does not happen due to an absence of political will at the top to make it happen. Promoters and top management get very enthusiastic about articulating the Identity & Covenant and generating statements and then lose steam when it comes to the actual work of aligning process by process without which no change will happen. Dedicated personnel are not assigned, and time and resources are not allocated and mixed messages are unconsciously (and sometimes consciously) given about the commitment of top management to the process of alignment.

For example in one BPO which had a problem of people working in silos and all decisions having to be taken by the founder CEO, a Steering Committee was formed with the specific goal of working together to take collective decisions. This is an excellent system that I have initiated in many companies and works wonders to ensure that information is shared, communication is improved, collaboration is automatic and the CEO is freed of all day to day decision making. However in the case in point the CEO attended the first meeting of the Steering Committee and spoke highly of the need for the Steering Committee. But as the meeting was about to close he said, "All right, ladies and gentlemen, please ensure that all decisions you take are cleared with me first before implementing." That was like shooting the thing in its head. The very purpose of the Steering Committee was vitiated and the intervention never achieved what it was intended to do and which it had done in many other companies with less insecure CEOs.

A second reason why alignment does not happen is because not enough attention is given to people's anxiety about transition and change. It is assumed that since the top management is excited, this excitement permeates the entire organization. There are no reality checks, attempts to listen to people or to deal with real issues and things are pushed until they reach a stage where the 'compensating loop neutralizes the causal loop' (Senge – Systems Thinking). It is essential to keep this in mind.

Causal & Compensating Loops

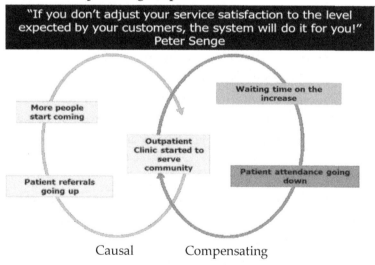

Causal   Compensating

For those who may not be familiar with the theory of Causal & Compensating Loops, here is a quick overview.

Example: A clinic is started to serve the community in a small country town. People are delighted and patient referrals to the clinic start to increase. More and more people start coming to the clinic instead of going to the hospital in the city. People from other nearby towns also start to come to this clinic as its reputation for good patient care spreads. This is the Causal Loop the desired end of which is to give good medical care to local people. Meanwhile as the patient load increases, so does waiting time. People start to complain about the long lines and the fact that often there are not enough places to sit, as the clinic never intended to have so many patients and so not enough seating was created when the clinic was built. There is pressure on the wash rooms and keeping them clean and sweet smelling becomes a challenge. Patients and their attendants get hungry and there is no restaurant nearby.

People start to bring their own snacks and drinks and this creates a problem of litter. All this is the Compensating Loop. After a while patient referrals decrease, fewer and fewer people come to the clinic and it falls into disuse. Undetected in time and unchecked, the Compensating Loop has the power to neutralize the positive effects of the Causal Loop and even to reverse its effect.

Communication is absolutely critical in getting alignment. Without proper communication, no alignment can happen and the anxiety will sabotage the entire change process. It is essential to keep an eye open for the start of the Compensating Loop and to neutralize it early before it has a chance to stop the Causal Loop. The classic example that I recall was of a large multi product manufacturing company in India where the Top Management declared in every meeting that merit would be the only deciding factor for career progress. However when it came to actually promoting people all kinds of factors including age, seniority, caste, personal contacts with the owner family members and so on were used to decide who would actually be promoted. It did not take too long for the loss of credibility to become visible to everyone except the people who were doing these things blissfully unaware or uncaring. Predictably with the departure of all those who had competence, entrepreneurship and integrity.

In another case a newly formed mobile phone services company in India started with lofty ideals of equality and freedom among employees. But unfortunately the American CEO who took charge turned out to be such a control freak that all creativity and spontaneity was quickly throttled and eventually 2 years later the company was acquired by another competitor. The way the morale of the staff got deflated was an amazing and very painful thing to see.

In both these instances the killer was the lack of congruence between what top management preached and what they actually did. What I call the **"negative differential between espoused and practiced values"**. Naturally no structures were created to ensure that what was espoused would actually be practiced since there was no real will to practice it. Most employees in general, are willing to believe top management pronouncements and invest a lot of emotional energy in propagating this message. That is why when they realize that the message was never seriously intended, the disillusionment is intense and very difficult to stem, much less turn back without a change in top management.

The cliché, "Trust is easy to destroy but difficult to rebuild," is never truer than in these cases.

Circle 3

Driving alignment through behavioral change
When embarking on the project of aligning organizational processes to the Identity & Covenant, it is essential to first identify the people who will be affected and ensure they understand what is happening and how it will help them. Helping people who are likely to be affected by the change to see what they will gain; is essential to getting their commitment. I have found that the most effective way is to simply have conversations in groups, facilitated by an external consultant, which explore in depth the meaning that the change has for people. Once they have a forum to talk about their apprehensions and expectations, the anxieties are laid to rest and the change process can start.

In many cases we have had simultaneous meetings with several selected opinion leaders across the organization and set up channels of communication to disseminate the Identity & Covenant to everyone. The only caveat at this stage is to remember that this is an 'informing' process where people have the choice to clarify understanding and commit to the Identity & Covenant. It is not an opportunity to rehash the Identity & Covenant. Highly skilful facilitation skill is necessary with the detachment that only a highly skilled outsider can bring. Often there is a high level of anxiety that needs to be dealt with and an external facilitator has a natural advantage which the organization can leverage. People at this stage have an opportunity to examine what the Identity & Covenant of the organization mean to them and to consciously decide to belong. The key is to do this consciously because only when the process is conscious does it 'bring tears to the eyes'. Emotional connection is essential to invoke the sense of pride and connectedness that I mentioned earlier.

People may ask questions to clarify their understanding and essentially decide to be in or out. But the Identity & Covenant will not be opened to changing at this stage for anyone. To choose to opt out of the organization is a possible outcome of this exercise for a very small number of people and should be accepted, even encouraged, as it preempts a lot of discord due to people who can't commit to the ideology while still being in the organization. This is often the hardest part especially when some of the people who opt out are otherwise good people. This stage is in my opinion a test of the measure of the CEO and Top Management and quite simply has within itself the roots of further success or failure. The single most damaging thing for the organization is to reach this stage and then fail to have the edge to part company with people who find it impossible to commit wholeheartedly to the Identity & Covenant. That is the acid test for the CEO. CEOs who fail to take decisive action have failed in their role and thereby doomed the entire process of building Enduring Leadership™.

Alignment: The key to smooth transition
Simultaneously with this conceptual buy-in process, the organization needs to dedicate a person (or more and with external help) to identify what processes need to be aligned and what specifically needs to be done to align them. Without alignment the benefits of the Identity & Covenant will never be realized and there will be eventual loss of credibility and destruction of morale.

Three questions must be answered for each process:

1. What needs to be aligned and why?
2. What will the new 'aligned' process look like?
3. How will you measure the level of alignment?

For example if recruitment is identified as a process to be aligned, the organization needs to justify it in terms of why it needs alignment. Then they have to conceptualize the new 'aligned' way in terms of what the new process will be. For example, what questions will be asked in an interview; will other methods be used apart from the interview to verify the information the candidate gives and so on. A whole set of questions will have to be created to ascertain if the candidates share the organization's core values. Then measurement metrics for the new system must be agreed upon to know that the new aligned system is actually functioning.

Similarly if teamwork is identified as a process to be aligned then compensation must be examined to see if it supports teamwork or competition. Team bonuses must be examined as a possible alternative to the standard individual scale. Performance assessment must be designed in a way to capture effective team working. Team roles must be assigned in keeping with people's preferences. Teaming skills training must be given to ensure that everyone is on the same page with respect to working on teams.

Alignment is essential simply because without it, the power of the Covenant will never be tapped. The values of the Identity will remain at the intellectual level and will never be seen in practice. The culture will not reflect the stated values and there will be a catastrophic loss of credibility and morale. It is this phase of alignment that is the make or break of the entire process orientation intervention. With proper alignment the organization will transform. Without it the organization will not simply remain where it was, but will actually get damaged by the resultant loss of credibility. For obvious reasons it is also wise to ensure that alignment is done soon after the Identity & Covenant clarification while the enthusiasm is still high.

The Intersection of Circles

Culture Supporting Alignment by Training, Measuring, and Rewarding

For each of the processes that are to be aligned specific Moments of Truth must be identified and monitored. It is by looking at how these are handled that gives us an idea about how well the new process is working. Monitoring Moments of Truth is essential to ensure that alignment is happening.

The 3 defining questions that must be posed and answered are:
1. What are the Moments of Truth that will indicate that your Culture is aligned to your Identity & Covenant?
2. What is the process to monitor them?
3. What are the metrics to measure them?

Measurement is very important as otherwise you don't have any idea if alignment is actually happening or not. Parameters have to be identified for each process and time periods for measurement, set.

For example in DHL, India the parameter for answering the telephone was set at two rings meaning that the phone would be answered on the second ring. This was to make sure that the ring was actually for DHL and that the wait for the customer was not too long. Another parameter was that the person answering the phone would handle the customer's query without transferring them to someone else. Now obviously if you set this parameter then you have to ensure that the frontline individual has access to all relevant information and is sufficiently empowered to take decisions to satisfy the client. So as I have mentioned in detail earlier, aligning a process to the Identity & Covenant can often entail restructuring systems, training, upgrading/designing technology to assist the individual to perform, new reporting relationships, changed levels of authority, fresh policy on information sharing and decision making and so on.

Many times before any alignment can be done, family/top management have to make some serious changes in their own approach and behavior. It is essential to directly face these facts and consciously choose to change. This is the hardest to do especially for the older members who may not want to change their ways with the excuse that their old way has worked well enough until then. Excuses don't change facts. So change in attitude, mindset and behavior are all essential and have to start at the top. The single biggest boost to credibility is for people to see the CEO behaving differently. That tells them that the matter is serious enough for them to take note of. Otherwise they take their cue from the CEO and top management and will give as much seriousness to the process as they see their bosses doing.

Without that it is entirely unlikely that any real change will actually happen. I have seen several cases of structural changes being made and then all their benefits nullified because the family/top management treats the new systems with disdain, sarcasm and a lack of seriousness. Needless to say, the rest of the organization will take their cue from this behavior and the change will only be cosmetic and lose all credibility. Once the structural changes are in place, there is a need to train (indoctrinate even) people in the new ways. This must start with the induction of new people and continue into all ongoing training and Corporate Communication. This process is very important also to take care of the anxiety of change. The training can be done internally as well as with the help of external facilitators/trainers. The specific nature of the training will obviously differ depending on the needs but it is essential to chalk out a stage-wise training plan where each stage reinforces the previous one.

Reward systems must reinforce the new behavior and become a source of inspiration for others to follow suit. Rewards need to be exemplary and high profile so that people know what is going on. Total credibility in rewarding is also essential which means that rewards are strictly on merit and that **there is no "consolation or symbolic prize."** Also it means that the top management sets the standard in implementation and not in creating exceptions to the rules that they themselves have set.

These three processes of training, monitoring and rewarding support each other and the result is a culture that supports the Identity & Covenant.

Creating this culture is very essential as it becomes the single most important factor that attracts the kind of people the organization needs to actualize its vision. At the same time this culture becomes the testing ground for alignment at a personal level and people who have difficulty aligning will leave. In my view the operative culture of the organization is what someone who does not know the organization will see and feel if they walk into the premises. If that is in line with the Identity & Covenant then the alignment is successful. If not, more work needs to be done.

Two Key Structures for a Process Driven Culture

In order to create a process driven culture it is essential to defocus from the individual and focus on the collective without becoming mechanical and impersonal. The challenge is to retain the feel of personal loyalty and belonging while transferring the emotion to the organization. The most important step in this process is to open ownership to others by creating spaces for meaningful participation. When people have a say in how things are run, what decisions are taken, the direction that the business takes and the pace of its growth, they feel a part of the business and commit to its wellbeing. They are no longer 'outsiders' but by virtue of their role work like 'insiders'.

I have suggested two structures below which enable this to happen. Both have been tried and tested in multiple situations and work wonderfully well, **provided there is the political will at the top** to allow them to function both in word and in spirit.

The Executive Council (EC)

The Executive Council comprises of the heads of all businesses or SBU's and the heads of common shared services like finance, HR, Legal, Administration and so on. This is like an internal management board of the organization. One of the most common features of family businesses is that people work in silos and build personal empires resulting in duplicating of work and resources. Functional/Business heads are secretive and reluctant to share information with each other, much less 'answer' to each other about performance. This creates mutual suspicion and rancor especially if one questions another. In the absence of a formal structure the social structure operates in which for a younger person to question an older person is well nigh impossible. In a process driven organization the age of the individual is immaterial. The role is all that counts and as long as a person is in a particular role, they are expected to perform. A formal structure helps to bring about this change.

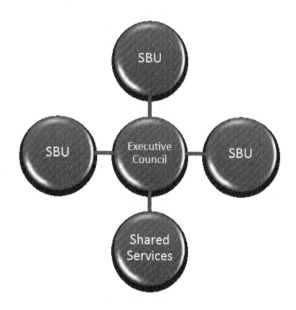

The Executive Council fulfils five critical purposes:
1. Share information across functions
2. Share decision making across functions
3. Make policy makers responsible for policy implementation
4. Preparing successors by giving them hands-on experience
5. Creating transparency, cooperation and collaboration

As I mentioned earlier, like a farmer's irrigation channel directs the water, a formal structure directs attention and energy where it will make the maximum impact and do the most good. Once people accept the structure then they will automatically behave in the way the structure guides them. That is why it is important.

The Executive Council is the body that enables, even mandates, the sharing of information. The members are all Functional/Business Heads. Each Functional/Business Head, at the monthly meeting presents an overview of their activity highlighting critical elements and asks for any help that they may need. This is an opportunity of on-going peer networking, sharing, rating and ensures cross functional communication. Sharing of information and collaboration becomes inevitable.

The second benefit is that all decision making is done mutually with everyone participating and offering solutions but the concerned Functional/Business Head takes the final call. There is a shared sense of responsibility for the decision which helps to bind the group together. This encourages, even enforces collaboration between individuals especially as there is the realization that everyone needs everyone else in order to succeed. The Executive Council leadership revolves (periodically) and so is not something that anyone has to fight for. The leader gets the cooperation of the others automatically as everyone realizes that one day their turn will also come when they will need the cooperation of the others.

The third benefit is that Executive Council members make policy and then are themselves responsible for implementing that policy in their own areas. This eliminates the problem of people feeling that policy is imposed on them by people who don't understand their particular difficulty. Having the Functional/Business Heads as the members of the EC ensures that they have a say in making the policy and are able to influence the process. Since they understand that they will have to implement whatever policy they make they ensure that all aspects are considered. Because they are involved in the whole process they are able to carry back to their functions/businesses, the big picture which will help others understand the rationale for the policy. Finally they will own accountability for implementation and be able to report back and ask for any help that they may need in implementation.

The fourth benefit of the Executive Council is that it is a place to groom successors for the Top Leadership of the organization. As I mentioned earlier, business leaders learn to do business by doing business. What better way to groom them than to give them decision making responsibility with the safety net of the advice and oversight of peers, each of whom has a stake in their success? The structure of the Executive Council ensures that all factors that have the potential to impact the decision are considered and then once the impact of the decision is felt, the decision is analyzed to see what can be learnt from it. Ill conceived plans and unsubstantiated risk are avoided.

The last and most important benefit of the Executive Council is the atmosphere of transparency, principle based questioning, objective decision making based on good information, teamwork and collaboration and offering and accepting help mutually that is created as a result of following this method of working. All these are critical issues in keeping business families together and tend to get neglected if there is no formal structure in place. Some families have informal structures which quickly degenerate into social fora that do little more than arrange family or company picnics and parties. The real sharing in business decision making never happens and people manage to still maintain unhealthy secrecy and build power bases that are detrimental for the family as a whole. The Executive Council eliminates all these negative tendencies and opens the door for openness and mutual cooperation.

It is interesting to remember that this form of collective decision making is nothing new. In India it is called the Panchayat and has been effective at the village level for more than 3000 years. In the Middle East it is a part of the Islamic system and is called the Majlis Ash-Shoora and is essentially the same structure where all key stakeholders sit together in a circle and elect one of themselves (usually the one who will be affected by the decision the most) as their leader (called Faisal) for that particular meeting. Then each presents his view with reasons and the Faisal makes the decision (called Fai-sala). This system has also been in existence for more than 1400 years. We even see evidence of this in the Bible in the stories of Moses and Jesus which means that it has been in existence for a few thousand years. There is something very powerful about all key stakeholders sitting in a circle and deciding on issues that affect them all. It is very primal, natural, logical, very human and very powerful. That is why the Executive Council is such a powerful structure and works so well.

Working Method
It is important for me to also narrate here the working method for the Executive Council. As I mentioned earlier, the leadership rotates and the leader for the meeting is the one who is most affected by the decision to be taken. Another way is to simply go round the table so that there is a new leader for each meeting. Whatever be the method, the point is that leading the Council is something that every member will inevitably do and so there is no need for any politics. Each person gets his or her opportunity

and so there is a vested interest for people to cooperate with the leader of the moment.

The leader has the right to ask anyone for advice and to take or not take the advice of anyone. He or she has the right to listen to everyone's advice and to come to his/her own conclusion. He has the right to state his/her opinion including stating what he/she can or can't change. However s/he must do all of this openly and in the meeting, not in the corridor or behind closed doors before the meeting.

The others must offer advice not from the perspective of their own narrow interest, convenience, likes or dislikes, but keeping in mind the interest of the whole family/business. This must be done even if it means inconveniencing themselves. They must offer their advice when asked and then be silent. They are welcome to offer clarifications, if asked. But on no account must they insist on or argue for their point of view. If their input is accepted they may feel happy but if it is not accepted they must not be resentful or feel bad about it. Their job was to offer their advice keeping the best interest of the whole family/business in mind. Once they did that their job is over. Finally and most importantly, once the leader takes the decision, the entire Executive Council must stand solidly and firmly behind the decision and the leader. Even those whose advice may not have been taken by the leader.

It is this unity of stance that is the most important element of ensuring mutual respect, appreciation and solidarity. The biggest harm is done when people sit silently or worse still, pretend to agree in the meeting and then criticize the decision when they go outside. That is tantamount to treason and undermines the authority of the Council to the detriment of all. That is the single most important behavior to avoid at all costs.

Venture Capital Fund
In the old days wise kings used to send off princes to earn their place by demonstrating their worth by doing some deed of valor. The one who was able to do the best was the one selected as the heir apparent to the king.

The second structure that I propose for business families is the Venture Capital Fund. It is true that a family member can always go to the family and ask for funds if he or she has a good business idea. But once again it is the power of the formalized structure that ensures that not only are good business ideas materially supported but the existence of a support structure will encourage ideas to come with regularity.

This is an excellent method to nurture future leadership, focus towards wealth creation and to keep alive the entrepreneurial spirit of the business. Anyone with a good business idea is welcome to present their Business Plan to an Assessment Committee which will evaluate the idea. This will be a formal assessment of the Business Plan by technical and financial experts as well as the family and if it is judged to be worthwhile the Committee will recommend it to the EC to finance it.

The Venture Capital Funding Process

Project Approval Process

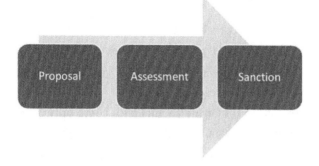

If not the Committee will tell the incumbent which areas need more clarity and which risks must be mitigated with good workable plans. The idea can then be presented again for another evaluation.

When a formal structure for funding new businesses is created it does many good things:

1. It keeps alive the spirit of entrepreneurship that is often the first casualty in business families that do well. This is paradoxical and very ironic but when the business does well the focus of the family shifts from creating new businesses to maintaining its existing business. From risk to safety, from conquering new frontiers to guarding old borders.
2. It lets people know that the family is open to the idea of new businesses and that the pie can be expanded. Expanding the pie is the best way to avoid intra-family conflict. When the business is big enough and expanding there is enough for everyone and there is no need for anyone to fight for a piece of the action. It is only when the pie is fixed that division becomes acrimonious.

3. It puts pressure on those who only talk (every family has some of these) to put their ideas where their mouths are. Nobody can complain that they did not get a chance and real leaders get visibility.
4. It creates a formal process of evaluation of ideas so that anyone whose idea is not accepted does not feel peeved about it but knows exactly where it fell short and what must be done to correct it and present it again.
5. It puts pressure on all family members to come up with new ideas on a regular basis. And like the processes in 3M for 'mandating innovation' the Venture Capital fund will 'mandate entrepreneurship'.

A final word on these two structures; even though the principal members and beneficiaries of these structures will be family members, I strongly advocate that they be open to anyone who makes the mark.

The Executive Council as I have conceptualized it here will have professionals on it as it is comprised on Functional and Business Heads. This is a very good thing as the family will benefit from the mindshare of people who have a wealth of experience especially from outside.

For the Venture Capital Fund, anyone in the business with a good idea must be able to present it to the Fund on the same terms as family members. This will create huge entrepreneurial energy and ensure that the family benefits from the ideas of everyone in the business. For businesses that are funded for non-family people, a shareholding pattern can be used where the family holds the major share (being the funder) and the initiator of the idea can hold a minor share and manage the business. That way the initiator of the idea can enjoy the benefits of owning his own business while remaining with the family instead of setting up outside as a competitor.

ENDURING LEADERSHIP™
INDIVIDUAL EXCELLENCE MODEL

"Our legacy is the memory we leave behind in the hearts and minds of people. People remember us not by what we consumed, but by what we contributed. It is up to us to decide what difference we want to make."

Developing Individual Leadership

No discussion of this nature can be complete unless we have a plan for developing the leadership that we hope will ensure that the organization outlasts its founders. And to do it in a way that is ongoing and sustainable. I have suggested a model to do this and can say with the confidence of practical experience that if this method is followed then the organization will truly be on the way to enduring greatness long after the founders have passed on.

Before I start on the model, I must mention a key attitude without which no progress is possible. And that is the Willingness to Learn. A hunger for knowledge, self development and self improvement where a person always asks the question, "What did I learn today?" It is amazing how much of learning is an everyday thing. That comes simply if one is focused towards learning. Like the famous line of Sherlock Holms, the detective, "I saw it because I was looking for it." The leader needs to be looking for learning. And when you are seeking to learn, it happens in the most odd and ordinary of situations. One of my most significant life learnings happened in India while buying some wheat in a small village shop.

Let me describe it to you.

Have you ever seen a traditional weighing scale in a shop in India selling food grains? It is called a 'Balance' and has two pans on either side of a pivot, hanging from a horizontal beam at the top. The weight measure is put in one pan and material being weighed in the other. There is an extremely important life lesson to be learnt in this. The next time you go to buy rice or some other grain, notice what the seller does. So for example if you ask him to give you 20 kilograms of wheat, he will first put a 20kg weight in one pan of the scale.

That pan now sits firmly on the counter top with the 20kg weight in the bottom. Then he starts to pour the grain into the other pan. In the beginning, since you want to buy a large quantity, he uses a scoop to get the grain from the sack in which is rests and pours it into the pan of the scale. He pours in scoop after scoop but nothing happens. The pan with the weight continues to sit firmly on the countertop. 15kg, 16kg...19kg; no movement, no change in the situation. But the man does not stop pouring in the grain. He does not give up because he does not see any change even after having worked so hard. He continues to do his job and keeps adding more and more grain.

And then you see the miracle, the inevitability of destiny. As he continues to add grain to the pan, when it is nearing 20 kilos, there is a tremor in the pan which has the weight. The shopkeeper now pours very carefully and the pan with the weight starts to rise. At that time the shopkeeper changes his method. Now instead of using the container to pour the grain he uses his hand. He holds a handful of grain and gently puts in a few grains at a time. And then lo and behold, the pan with the grain starts to get heavier and the pan with the weight rises in the air.

I have described this process in so much detail because this simple action which we in India and perhaps in many other parts of the world have seen many times, establishes two critically important principles for me.

1. Until 19.9 kg nothing will happen
2. After 19.9 kg the scale **will tip over**

Both are unchanging and inimitable principles of life. Both are equally true. This is a turning point. Until that point is reached, there is no visible difference in the situation. But if we continue our effort in good faith and refuse to be discouraged, then it is equally true that the scale **WILL** tip over in our favor.

That nothing will happen until 19.9 and that after 19.9 the scales will tip over, are both equally true.

So when in the late reaches of the night I am feeling discouraged, exhausted with the effort of apparently endless striving without visible results, I always try to remind myself of this principle and recall the little exercise of buying food grain to help me to reinforce my spirit. By asking myself this question, 'What can I learn from this?' I have been able to get some significant learning from many otherwise ordinary, even mundane situations.

There is a very fine theory explained by David Kolb which explains this entire process of learning from life. It is called the Theory of Adult Learning. The key is to practice this consciously ensuring that each of the stages described is actually gone through.

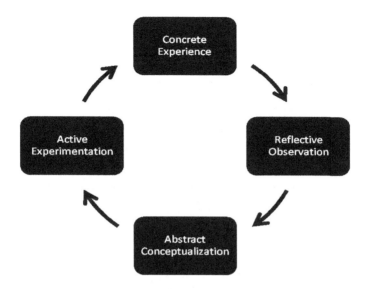

The theory is that in the beginning is the actual experience that one has; called the **Concrete Experience**. When one is in it, it's essential to have a high degree of self awareness because all data for further learning will come from this. One needs to be aware of one's attitude, feelings, mental models, motivations and changes in all of these as the incident unfolds. Once the incident is over then one takes some time out for quiet reflection about what happened which Kolb called **Reflective Observation**. It is a wonderful phrase which describes the process of re-living the incident. Of playing back the memory to 'see' what happened in your mind's eye. To analyze what actually happened and what could have happened if you had done some things differently. Of owning your responsibility in it.

Without owning responsibility you have no power to change outcomes. That is why people who run away from responsibility are powerless to change their future. They choose to be victims of circumstances because they are afraid of owning responsibility for their own role in what happened. Consequently they are denied the power to change those circumstances. It is essential to understand that no matter what the situation and whatever be your role in it, there will always be things in your control and things that are outside your control. That is why my maxim in life is: **"I will not allow what is not in my control, to prevent me from doing what is in my control."** During the phase of Reflective Observation one owns responsibility and does a lot of 'what-if' thinking.

From this phase comes the phase of learning a lesson which Kolb called **Abstract Conceptualization.** This in simple terms is what we call, 'Learning a lesson'. This is perhaps the most critical phase of learning. Unless one can conceptualize experience, one learns nothing. Raw experience in merely data. Nothing more. It is, by itself not useful even to the one to whom it happened. That is why many people repeat mistakes, because they have not learnt anything from what happened to them. If one can conceptualize experience then one not only learns but one can also teach the lesson to others using one's own life as the canvas on which to paint the picture. People find personal life histories the easiest lessons to relate to and resonate with your learnings because they can find similar incidents in their own lives.

Finally the test of the pudding; applying the learning. For it is only in the application that the learning manifests its benefit. This Kolb calls **Active Experimentation.** Experimentation is about the courage to act. To put one's judgment on the line. To try out what one believes in and to prove the concept. This is what builds credibility in the end. The actual proof that your method works. When people can see the benefit themselves they don't need any more convincing. This is what active experimentation does. It demonstrates proof of concept.

When you don't go through all the stages of learning...

People don't benefit in the same way even though they may have experiences which are similar because they don't go through the Adult Learning Cycle in a structured manner. They short circuit one or the other stage with corresponding mistakes in learning. For example, if they are not conscious of their feelings, thoughts and situation completely when they are in the Concrete Experience stage, the data that they have for analysis in the next stage is faulty or deficient. Consequently the results will be faulty. In the next stage even if the data is good, but if they get stuck in merely Reflective Observation, they will probably dwell too long on what happened without deriving any learning from it. This brooding can send the individual into a depression as well if the incident they are brooding on is negative. Or if the incident was enjoyable, it simply gives them a nice warm happy feeling without any learning to show at the end of it.

Sometimes people jump directly to the Abstract Conceptualization stage from Concrete Experience. This is the cause of all stereotypes and prejudice. Finally some people never get up the courage to try out their learning, even though they may have understood the situation well and formed a good concept for the future. That is a great pity because it is only in the action that theory shows its worth. But if you never implement the lesson, no benefit can accrue. It is a very important thing therefore to ensure that you follow the entire cycle completely.

The thing to remember when learning is that if one is indeed practicing the new way, then one's efficiency is bound to suffer initially. Then when you start becoming proficient in the new way efficiency will increase and go beyond its earlier levels. But in the beginning as soon as you start practicing the new way, it will drop. This is the area of pain.

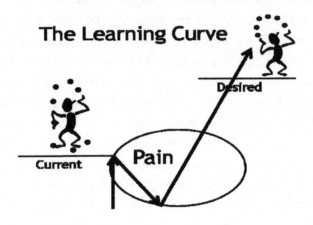

Many people become impatient and give up the new way because they are unable to go through the area of pain. It is easy to see this for example when learning a new language. We start off with enthusiasm but as mastering the grammar and acquiring sufficient vocabulary is simply a matter of memorizing, which many people find difficult to do, we give up. As a result we may have a few words or phrases of the new language but never really become proficient in it. That is why perseverance is an essential ingredient of all learning.

Perseverance is a derivative of resilience. Winning is nothing more than rising every time you fall. **Resilience** is a process which I have illustrated below.

The first step in Resilience is to face facts squarely. Not with rose colored glasses or fantasies about how 'somehow' everything will be well. But by understanding the gravity of the situation. Many studies with inmates of concentration camps have shown that those who survived did not expect to be rescued next week or next month, or by some outside force or miracle. They accepted clearly the fact that they were in a terrible, life threatening situation and took steps to deal with it, physically and psychologically. Those who expected quick rescues gave up hope and died when the rescue did not happen at the time that they expected. Needless to say these learnings are not for concentration camp inmates alone.

In business as well, when things fail people tend to lose hope and react by becoming overly cautious and losing growth opportunities because they fail to take risk at the right time.

So the first step is not to fool yourself or to fantasize about the gravity of the problem. Instead one must face it, analyze it, understand it fully and above all, to accept that it is something that affects us deeply and significantly. Paradoxically it is also essential to believe in your ultimate success because unless you believe that you will be successful it will be impossible to get up from failure. Sometimes this faith in eventual success may not even seem logical, with little or no evidence to point to it. However people who have eventually succeeded have been those who still believed that they would succeed even when others around them started to lose hope. The final step in this sequence is to make a clear plan of action to take you out of your difficulty.

Even though there will always be an element of the 'unknown' in how events transpire and results happen, much of it is logical cause and effect. So if one plans well and anticipates eventualities, then one is prepared for them and in the end the result is as one would have wished. Structured planning with time lines and metrics to measure progress are the key to success. Planning and structured action succeeds where mere inspiration peters out.

The Individual Excellence model

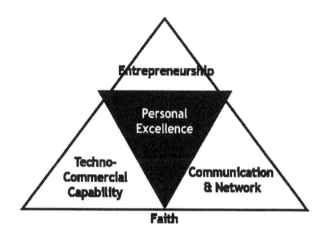

Enduring Leadership™ is a core of **Personal Excellence**, arising from the bed-rock of values grounded in **Faith**. This core supports the spearhead of **Entrepreneurship** while itself being supported on the one side by **Techno-Commercial Capability** and on the other side by **Communication & Network.**

The purpose of the model for Individual Development is to enable the organization to drive alignment through training and development of its people. It is important therefore to be clear about what the final product will look like. The model defines the core competencies that are needed.

Faith
Small word with big meaning. Means different things to different people. So let me define what I mean by 'Faith'. To me, faith is a dynamic process that is based on the individual's understanding of him/herself in the context of physical, intellectual, psychological and spiritual strength. That is why self awareness

and emotional understanding is very important. Based on this s/he takes risk and has success which reinforces the faith. When there is a failure, if they analyze it and create a new strategy that also reinforces the faith. Otherwise, faith can be shaken sometimes with failures.

Faith is the sure knowledge that one will succeed in one's endeavor. To do all that is required and then to trust that the result will be favorable. This may sound irrational. But it is a very critical element of the combination. It is the final ingredient in the mix that produces success. Without faith you reach the end of your strength and find nothing to sustain you across the leap...the leap of faith.

I like to use the words of Barbara Winters to describe faith: "When you come to the end of the light of all that you know and are about to step off into the darkness of the unknown, faith is knowing that one of two things will happen; there will be something firm to stand on, or you will be taught how to fly."
For me faith is knowing with complete certainty that Allah will do what He promised in the Qur'an: Sura At-Talaaq: 2-3: "For the one who has consciousness of Allah (and fears His displeasure – has taqwa) Allah will extract him from all his difficulties. And will provide him from sources that he could not imagine. For the one who has faith in Allah, verily He (Allah) will become sufficient for him."

It is this faith that gives courage. The courage to take the unpopular stance. To speak the truth before the tyrant. To stand up for the oppressed. To do what needs to be done no matter how difficult, to follow your dream. It is this faith that lights the path on the long, dark road in the late reaches of the night when all about you are asleep and you are sitting wondering if the road that you have chosen to walk is really worth it or not. When human awareness and resistance to adversity is at its lowest, faith is the small, clear voice in your heart which tells you that what you are doing is right and gives you the courage to carry on.

Personal Excellence

From the foundation of faith arises an ever-expanding band of rays. The light of **Personal Excellence.** This is a standard that the person holds himself to irrespective of whether or not anyone else appreciates or agrees. This standard defines the individual and determines his success or failure.

Personal Excellence to me is a combination of 3 factors:

Clarity of Purpose: What exactly do you want to achieve?

It is very important to define the goal as clearly as possible. It must be clear, not need long explanations, excite the imagination and create even some apprehension about the individual's ability to succeed. The ability to clearly visualize the outcome, to conceptualize the final product, to literally see it, feel it, taste it, invokes enormous energy. The degree to which one can visualize the end, to that degree is one motivated to achieve it.

The differential between current reality and the ultimate goal creates a positive stress that produces the energy needed for the surge in effort necessary to succeed. The bigger the goal, the scarier it is, the more it will motivate. It is in the nature of extraordinary goals to inspire extraordinary effort. The person standing at the foot of Mount Everest, intending to scale its peak is frightened but the fear does not send him back home. It energizes and excites him. The prospect of standing on the top of the mountain keeps him going during the dark and difficult periods, through the ice and snow, braving the winds and conquering the pain and exhaustion in his own body. The goal is difficult but it is clear. That clarity is most important.

To develop this clarity, writing is very important. An exercise I do is to give people large sheets of newsprint (chart paper) and crayons or paints. Then I ask them to draw their lives, starting from their earliest memories. I tell them to draw these pictures in any order they please and to group them chronologically. Once they have done the drawings I ask them to identify the thresholds or places of movement where they feel they moved ahead in life. This movement may have been in any form, psychological (breaking a mental barrier), financial, material, hierarchical, relationship-wise or anything else. Once they have identified their thresholds, I ask them to reflect on what they are seeing in their own life story. I ask them to identify their strengths, weaknesses, the good decisions they took and why, the mistakes they made and the learnings from them. When they have completed this exercise (and this may well take several hours) I ask them to try to visualize what the future seems to hold for them.

I remind them that we are responsible for and free to make any choice we wish. Once we make the choice, its consequences will unfold. It is like going out of the gate of your home and taking a right or a left turn. You have no control over what you will see once you take the turn. You will see whatever is along the road in that direction. You can't change what is along the road. But you can choose which direction to take; right or left. Life is like that. We are free to choose. But the choices have consequences. Not making a choice also has consequences which are sometimes more expensive than making a choice. But just like while driving, if we discover that we took the wrong turn, all we need to do is to simply turn around and go back to the intersection and take the correct turn. In most cases in life, we have the freedom to make a U-turn. I am not saying that it is always easy. But it is possible.

From this exercise people are able to arrive at what they see as the purpose of their lives. I tell people that while it is indeed true that you are not compelled to live your life purposefully, it is a wonderful thing to live a life that counts. Otherwise there is really no essential difference between a human being and any animal. After all animals also eat, drink, make babies and die. Not having left any sign of their passing. In my view a person who lives without purpose, lives essentially an animal life. For a human being, if someone said, "So what if he lived?" ... there should be an answer. If one has to say, "So nothing!!" then that is an animal life. A mechanical existence which wasted all the resources that went into making it possible and which left no legacy of its passing. Such a person may just as well, not have been born. A clear Life Purpose saves us from this oblivion and ensures that when we are gone, we will be remembered with honor for the legacy we left behind.

Once this purpose is clearly defined please do the **SMART** test on it.
Is the goal a **SMART** goal?
- **S:** Specific (Clear definition that needs no explanation)
- **M:** Measurable (what are the metrics to measure its accomplishment?)
- **A:** Actions (What do you need to do to achieve the goal?)
- **R:** Reasonable (Is it feasible? It may be challenging but is it doable at all?)
- **T:** Time (By when do you expect to achieve it?)

To convert an intention into a goal it is essential to make it SMART. Otherwise intentions remain nebulous and unachievable because not enough mindshare has gone into how exactly they are to be achieved. We often express goals in terms of 'Being' statements. "I want to be this or that". But to Be you have to Do. So all 'Being' statements must be reduced to 'Doing' statements. What do you have to do in order to be? It is good to remember that to Be, you have to Do. But to Do, you don't have to wait to Be. And unless you Do, you will never Be. So 'Being' goals must be translated into 'Doing' goals with a clear roadmap and time lines for achievement.

Workable Strategy: How will you achieve it?
The next step is to devise a workable strategy to achieve the goal. This has to take into account all the resources required to achieve it and have as clear a time line as possible to monitor progress. It must indicate who will be responsible for what task and must have the buy-in of the individual concerned. The more detailed the strategy the easier it will be to implement it. These details are not to make it rigid. They are to ensure that you have taken into

account all the elements that are necessary to succeed and that you have created a contingency plan in case it fails.

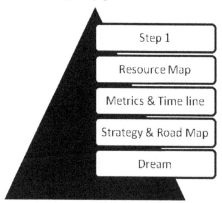

Strategy is the way you plan to go about accomplishing your Life Purpose. It is the method as well as the overall planned framework. The strategy must be tested either through a pilot or conceptually and checked with those who have experience to ensure that it is feasible. It can be ambitious, even scary. But it must have a reasonable chance of succeeding.

Out of the strategy comes the next step; the Road Map. The road map clarifies the steps you need to take in order to achieve your goal. It also specifies the metrics to measure progress, the Milestones. Without measurement parameters, hard work assumes the place of results and intension masquerades as achievement, until one day the individual wakes up to the reality that the dream is still a dream. So metrics are very important. The most important of the metrics is the time frame in which the goal is to be achieved. Each milestone must be described on two planes: quantum and time. How much, by when? This will tell us how successful or otherwise our efforts have been. The rule of thumb in this is that even a poor measurement is better than no measurement. Because a measurement gives you a parameter to judge progress. Without measurement you can never tell if your effort is bearing fruit or not.

The other even bigger danger of working without measurement is that one can get deceived by the effort alone and lose track of the goal. So, as I mentioned earlier, activity takes the place of purpose and being busy becomes an end in itself. One does not stop to ask what the result of being busy was. This false sense of progress is very harmful because in the end the goal is not achieved and all the efforts and resources that went into the project would have been wasted. We see so many examples of well meaning people making a lot of effort, expending a lot of passion and emotional capital but doing it in an unstructured, disjointed manner where it gets vitiated and has no leverage. After some time they lose enthusiasm and become bitter about the goal itself or with their teams or themselves. The fault however was in none of these things but in their approach to the project which was not systematic. The system I have described here will save you from this kind of disappointment.

After the Roadmap/Metrics and Timeline comes the Resource map which is the investment that one needs to make in the vision. This investment can be monetary and material or it can be in terms of emotional, mental and intellectual energy and effort. More often than not, it is the latter which is more difficult. Self development is an essential pre-requisite to career development. Resources are also in the form of key people whose help you may need as mentors, guides or coaches. You need to identify them, talk to them and get their agreement to help you so that when you actually need them, they are available to you and are willing to give time.

Once this planning is done, then you are ready to take the first step forward.

Will to Follow Through: Do you have the determination to do whatever it takes?

The third circle is about the will to see the endeavor through to completion. All great goals consist of a few moments of excitement followed by long hours of dull, mundane, back breaking sweating without which the final glorious success will never come. It is this period of high effort and little visible result that is the biggest hurdle to most endeavors. There are two secrets to get through this period:

1. Periodic and repeated reminders about the final objective
2. Celebrating small successes.

Rituals like the Wal-Mart chant which may seem silly to outsiders are a way of achieving both the reminding as well as celebrating success. Consistency is essential in this. It is said that Sam Walton always ended every store visit by leading a chant. Remember that this is not about the chant per se. The Wal-Mart chant is very American in terms of its cultural flavor and would look very odd in other cultures. So do something that is acceptable in your culture. But do it. And do it consistently. That is essential.

A Wal-Mart story on celebrating success is as follows: Opening new stores was intrinsic to the Wal-Mart strategy of cutting costs and margins and maximizing volume. More stores mean more volume. So Sam would fly low over farming towns to look for likely locations for his stores. Once he found a place between two or three towns, he would land and buy the piece of farmland and his 'troops' would set up a store as simply as rolling out a carpet. They had the whole business of setting up a store reduced to a measurable process and went about it like a well run machine. One tradition that went with this was that once the store was ready to be opened, Sam Walton and the Directors of Wal-Mart would personally serve a barbeque meal to those who had worked on the store setting up.

Essentially this included everyone from the hole digger to the pole cutter to the roof layer to the store manager.

A story written on the Wal-Mart site by one of these so-called 'lowly' workers goes that in one place the store was finally ready at 2.00 am. As they finished the work what do they see? They see Sam and some of his Directors roll up in their cars, pull out the makings of a barbeque and they had a party right there and then at 2.00 am, served by Sam and his partners on the board. 30 years after the event this incident is the highlight in the heart of the writer (and no doubt many others) which she remembered with affection and pride. **There's nothing small about celebrating small successes.** It is a very big thing with far reaching positive effects. People like to be appreciated and it is essential to do it regularly and frequently; and more importantly, consistently.

Teaching Personal Excellence
Personal excellence is taught by demonstration. I recall an incident today more than 40 years after it happened which taught me the lesson of demonstrating personal excellence by personal practice. I was in Standard 8 (12 years old) and it was a few minutes before the recess when I looked out of the window and to my astonishment, I saw our school's Principal, Mr. K. Kuruvilla

Jacob with a bucket with brushes in one hand and a broom in the other, walking into the toilets that were opposite my class. Mr. Jacob was a tall handsome man, very dark in complexion and always wore white trousers, a white bush-shirt and very highly polished black leather shoes. He always had a smile on his face and in my 12 years in school I don't remember ever seeing him angry about anything. Not that we did not do our best to give him cause.

Ours being a typical boys school, the toilets were the site of much prose and poetic expression, all uniformly unspeakable. Not very nice. Just then, as he disappeared into the toilets, the bell rang and all of us boys silently walked out and stood in a huddle before the toilets to see what the Principal was up to. While we watched, he quietly washed all the writing from the walls of the toilet and cleaned the toilets and then without saying a single word to us, went back to his office. I was in that school for 4 years after this incident and can vouch for it that nobody ever wrote anything on the toilet walls again.

Personal excellence is taught by demonstration and that is very powerful. People get a sense of pride that is associated with their identity and this is a great motivator. How you talk to people, deal with customers, drive on the road, pay your suppliers, answer the phone, treat your family and keep yourself, your home, your toilet and your business premises, all announce to the world your commitment to personal excellence. No amount of talking about personal excellence can beat the power of one single incident.

Someone told me a story about Nelson Mandela (Madiba) which illustrates this point of demonstrating personal excellence. The story goes like this: The President of a large multinational company which was doing some work in rural and social development wanted an appointment with Mr. Mandela. After a long wait due to Mr. Mandela's schedule he eventually managed to get a breakfast appointment. That morning as his driver drove up the driveway and pulled up in the porch of the house, the man was astonished to see Mr. Mandela waiting for him at the bottom of the stairs. The man was very honored and delighted at this great courtesy. As they sat down to breakfast, Madiba asked him, "Weren't there two of you in the car?" The man replied, "Yes Sir. The other man is my driver." Madiba excused himself, got up from the table and went out and shortly ushered the driver into the room and had him sit down to eat with himself and the head of the company. The breakfast went off well. Mr. Mandela made no mention about bringing in the driver.

Shortly thereafter Mr. Mandela's two guests left. As they reached the office of the company and the corporate head got out of his car, the driver came around and shook his hand and said, "Sir, I want to thank you specially for inviting me to eat breakfast with Mr. Mandela. It has been my dream to meet the great man but I have not been able to do that until today. Today thanks to your invitation, not only did I meet him but I was able to have breakfast with him. I had not even dreamt that I, a poor driver, would ever have this opportunity. So I want to thank you very much."

The company head was astonished to hear this. He said to his driver, "Why do you say that I invited you?" The driver replied, "Mr. Mandela came out and said to me, 'Your boss wants you to come in and eat with us.'"

This story illustrates for me how one's commitment to personal excellence lights the lives of others.

Entrepreneurship

I believe that the entrepreneurial spirit in the business which was at its start-up phase must never be allowed to evaporate or change. It is this speed of response, risk taking attitude, willingness to take ownership and personal relationships with customers that is the surest guarantee of success and growth. How does one develop entrepreneurial thinking? What are its benefits? Anyone can be entrepreneurial. You don't need to be a business owner. Anyone at any level can be, provided they decide to take responsibility for themselves, their words and their actions. Provided they stand up, willing to be counted. 'You will never amount to anything until you are willing to be counted', as some wise person said.

I have conceptualized my understanding of what it is to be entrepreneurial as follows: Entrepreneurship is all about ownership and responsibility. Ownership for our actions and their consequences. Therefore the willingness to speak and act responsibly. Entrepreneurship is perhaps the only quality that is close to being a 'universal formula of success' in the organization. It is the quality that brings the employee closest to the world of the employer because it helps him to transition from 'employee thinking' to 'owner thinking'.

The entrepreneur is distinguished from the 'bureaucrat' because he is in actual touch with the customer. S/he takes decisions. The entrepreneur does what it takes to make the customer happy. The entrepreneur is concerned if the customer is not happy and goes out of the way to make sure that the customer comes back. All this because s/he is totally convinced that the customer is not a nuisance or a necessary evil but the very cause of his/her own survival and growth.

Entrepreneurs are clear about the importance of customers and their satisfaction and that they themselves need to do everything in their power to ensure that this satisfaction index does not drop. However as businesses grow and employees increase, a gradual distancing from the customer ensues. It is almost as if success is the enemy of success and within it holds the seeds of failure. The bigger the organization, the more distant it tends to get from those it seeks to serve. Especially its top management. And that is the beginning of the decline.

Entrepreneurial spirit as defined in the Enduring Leadership™ model is the willingness to be accountable. The willingness to say, 'I am responsible and I want you to count on me.' The willingness to treat failures as learning opportunities. The willingness to share success with others who helped to make it happen and the personal rigor to own responsibility for failure. An attitude of being fanatically results driven with the readiness to do what it takes to succeed, no matter how difficult.

Interestingly as I mentioned earlier this entrepreneurial spirit is the first casualty of success and growth of the organization. The focus, even of the founder/group is towards seeking safety, creating bureaucracy in the name of management control and self aggrandizement to reflect their new status of eminence. Risk taking, delegation of responsibility, openness of approach and the personal touch with the customer all either take second place or disappear altogether with predictable results.

Techno-commercial Capability

Techno-commercial capability is that which converts a good idea into a good business. People who have this expertise are able to identify business opportunities where others see only mundane boredom. It is to be able to see opportunity and to use it to commercial advantage.

I remember listening to an elderly gentleman, himself a very wealthy man with huge property holdings in Central Bombay; tell me the story of how his father built his huge timber business in the 1900's.

He said to me, "My father was a stevedore in the docks in Bombay during the British colonial period. Along with other laborers he used to unload ships which docked in Bombay Port. These ships used to bring finished goods, mainly cloth from Manchester, to India. These bales of cloth would be placed on shelves in the hold of the ship. After unloading their cargo the captains would simply throw away the planks of which the shelves were made. They did this because from India they would take back cotton, indigo, wheat and other commodities which simply went into the hold and were not placed on shelves. My father noticed that these planks were made of Burma teak wood and having been in the hold, wet and dry for months, they were well seasoned. Well seasoned Burma teak is a very valuable wood, so my father went to the captain and asked if he could arrange for the clearing out of the holds at his expense provided he could take the planks. The captain agreed. And thus was born one of the most successful ship chandler businesses in India which had a very neat ancillary in timber and wood working." All about recognizing a business opportunity while others in the same environment don't.

In the context of my model for individual development this also refers to being known as an expert in your core area and then be able to use that expertise to help others achieve the common goal.

Communication & Network
Can you recruit helpers in this goal? As we accomplish our objectives through others, it is essential to be able to influence. Communication & Network is all about influencing. Who is willing to follow your lead? This depends on who is inspired by our vision and is willing to commit to the fulfillment of our cause. Can you show people what's in it for them? That is the operative question, the only station that all people listen to is WiiFM (What's in it for me?) Can you create a network of motivated helpers spanning continents who are willing to do what it takes to enable our goals to be achieved? The skills required to build this network and to be able to speak publicly such that people will be willing to commit time and resources to your cause is a critical leadership skill.

To do that you need to be able to communicate with passion. Without people who share the same passion and are willing to make the same commitment, the noblest goals remain mere ideas. The key to igniting the passion of others is to be so passionate about the idea yourself that when you speak, your passion is like a fire coming out of a flame thrower. It ignites everything in its path and lights the way for all to see. The heart of leadership is the ability to inspire others, to create followers. To inspire people around a simple powerful stretch goal. To enable them to dream your dream and to see how they will personally benefit if they follow you as their leader. To be able to touch their hearts. To convey the vision in language that they can relate to.

To get teams to pull together. To be able to resolve conflicts. To communicate with passion is the key element in influencing. To be able to influence others it is essential for one to be open to influence oneself. Strange as it sounds unless you are open to others you will not be able to influence them. Openness begets openness and when you are open to people they will listen to you. This is the first requirement for influencing – be open to others.

The second key to influencing is to show genuine concern for others. As the saying goes, "They don't care what you know, until they know that you care." So being genuinely interested in people, concerned for them and willing to do what it takes to help them, enables you to become highly influential. Genuineness is the key in this whole affair. Acting cannot be sustained. You can't pretend to be interested or concerned about others when you are in fact only concerned about yourself. We can easily judge the sincerity of others when they talk to us. So can they judge our own. And they will. And they will be closed to your influence. So being sincere, genuinely concerned is a key pre-requisite for anyone who wants to influence others.

The third key to influencing is to look for ways in which you can benefit others. This is yet another thing that may sound strange especially in a world where wanting to benefit anyone other than yourself is seen as foolish. But the fact of life is that when we get focused on benefiting others, we benefit ourselves, not only materially but also emotionally and spiritually.

I have practiced this in my life for decades very effectively. I give leadership seminars and workshops for schools, teachers, parent groups, religious and social welfare groups, free of cost. Last year (2007) that amounted to more than 60 working days. A very considerable time and monetary commitment on my part. However as a result, the kind of exposure and credibility that I earned in the business world was worth millions of dollars. If I had tried to advertise my expertise and service by paying for it, I would never have been able to afford it. But my work with these constituents who usually don't have the resources to afford my level of expertise got me the publicity and good will that nothing else could have done. It is true that I did not work with them for this purpose, but it is a benefit that I earned, nevertheless. Added to this was the enormous satisfaction of seeing the change in people's lives, effectiveness and relationships and knowing that I had been able to make a difference to enable them to be more happy, productive and powerful. Also the thought that my ideas and thoughts would be used and practiced in many parts of the world, all of which would never have happened if I had charged for these seminars.

Communication is about being believed. It is about building credibility and gaining positive visibility where your opinion is sought and people look to you for guidance. The leverage of influencing is to get those who you want to influence, to ask you, "Tell us what you want us to do." That is possible only when you can show them how they benefit from what you are suggesting. Authenticity is the key.

The good that you want them to see must actually be there. In the end however, people look at you more than they listen to what you suggest. You are who they believe. Building credibility is a long and slow journey.

Communication is also about being able to convey what you want to say in a clear, uncomplicated and inspiring manner. It is the ability to sense what will touch the hearts of the audience and to put things in that perspective. It is about knowing what to say, when to say, how much to say and when not to say anything at all. Communication is even more about listening. About listening to the words, to the feelings behind the words, to the anxieties and fears that may be between the lines and to the hopes and aspirations that are in the silence when all the talking is done. Communication is about speaking from the heart. It is about a high degree of congruence between thought, feeling and speech. It is about linking to people by being with them and for them when they need you the most. It is about putting people before yourself. It is about understanding that a leader is only as powerful as his followership. It is about understanding that even more than followers need a leader, the leader needs the followers. It is all about goodwill, which today even has a cash value. But cash value or not, goodwill is the measure of your leadership. How many people are willing to speak a good word for you? Especially in difficult situations, where to speak for you may put them in trouble. Yet they do it.

Communication is about understanding the value of the emotional bank account. Like in your monetary bank account, you put in the money when you don't need it, so that you will have it when you need it. In the emotional bank account you need to build the balance by helping people you don't need. Sometimes people you may never need. And you do this because you understand that the world is round and what goes around, comes around. This means that if you keep helping people when they need help, then one day when you need help someone will be sent to you. I say sent, because that is the only way to explain what happens. It is not the very people you helped, who will or even can help you when you need help. The nature and magnitude of what you need may be beyond them. But when you need it, it will come. And all that you will do is to stand by and watch in thankfulness and wonder at how things work out for you. All because you helped people without expecting any immediate return or payment. For there are many instances where people are leaderless. But none where there is a leader without followers. The word leader implies that there are followers. Without followers you would be alone. Not a leader. So communication and influencing is the very essence of being a leader. A leader that is a role model and an inspiration for others.

As I write about this model of personal development it is quite clear to me that it is a model of lifelong learning and development. It is not a model that one can say, "Well, I have arrived." It is an exciting look at life to see how one can continue to live it till the time comes to meet one's Creator, learning new things each day and contributing in new ways all along. Sometimes as a learner. Sometimes as a teacher. Sometimes simply as someone who watches from the sidelines as those he has prepared enter the competition of life to fight the good fight. For he also serves, who only bears witness. Personal development is partly about learning from others, teachers, mentors, role models. But even more, it is learning by yourself. By always asking the question, "So what is the lesson in this?"

I have practiced this all my life, thanks to my father's teaching and have always been amazed at all that can be learnt in the most simple and ordinary of situations. The situation is incidental. The learning is critical.

Achaaryaath paadam aadatthe

paadam sishya swamedhayaa
paadam sa brahmachaaribhya
sesham kaala kramena cha

This is the advice given in smruthies.

A person can get only one quarter of knowledge from the Achaarya, another quarter by analyzing self, one quarter by discussing with others and the last quarter during the process of living by method addition, deletion, correction, and modification of already known aachaaraas.

KEEPING THE FAMILY TOGETHER WHILE TRANSFORMING THE BUSINESS

"To leave behind a legacy that honors you long after you are gone. To create a system that each generation will hand down to the next in an unbroken chain of goodness. That to me is the true meaning of being 'The Best of People'. The best is the one who does the most good."

The Family Dynasty

As ownership passes from generation to generation, priorities change, complexity of opinions and pulls in different directions emerge and power dynamics change. Ownership patterns themselves may change with one branch of the family becoming more powerful than another. This may be for a variety of reasons, among them the availability of children to take charge, active involvement in the business, actually one branch or individual buying out others and some businesses in a group doing better than others. In the East dynamics of power and authority bestowed by society and religious tradition also play a significant role. For example in the traditional Hindu Joint Family the head of the family is called the 'Kartha' and is the final decision maker in all affairs. In the family business this person would typically be the Chairman of the Board. The Indian Income Tax Act recognizes the Hindu Undivided Family (HUF) as a single economic unit and the Kartha of the HUF is allowed to file one single tax return for the whole family, irrespective of how many earning members there may be in it. This is a major financial advantage which other religious groups are not given although the Joint Family is an Indian cultural construct and not limited to Hindus alone. Be that as it may the Kartha or Head of the Family has considerable authority simply by virtue of birth.

Usually 'Kartha-hood' is inherited by the oldest surviving male in the family. So it would be the brother of the Kartha, if he had any brothers or his oldest son. There is no guarantee however that he would have the same authority or acceptability that his predecessor had. People are different and so is their ability to inspire followership. However in business families, money plays a big role and so the most active person in the business will have an advantage. There are cases where the role of the Kartha was divided in a business family (Murugappa case) with the oldest sibling being the Kartha for family matters but his younger brother, more capable in business, being the Chairman of the Board. In other cases this transition is not handled with the same level of maturity and the result is not pretty. Irrespective of the way the transitions are done, there is a significant change in power dynamics which must be allowed for and dealt with. Interestingly the process that I have described above is the same in Muslim families in India and the Middle East as well, though the term 'Kartha' is not used. For example the system of succession in the Saudi Royal Family follows the same process with one brother after another inheriting the throne, after the death of their father HM King Abdul Aziz Ibn Saud.

In the East, the transition of 'Generations' in terms of power and say in matters is not always clear nor neatly divided into 'Founder – Sibling Partners – Consortium of Cousins' as John Ward suggests about Western business families, in his work. In my experience, family businesses work more like the diagram below with two or more generations participating at any given moment and an overlap in authority.

The reason for this is simple. In India, the Middle East and Africa when someone starts a business his whole family gets involved. Firstly because families tend to be close knit, the meaning of 'family' itself is different from the West. In the East family means almost anyone related in some way or the other, including through marriage. Family members get involved also because money supply is strained and family members are the only ones who will work for next to nothing except hope. Also trust is usually not in plentiful supply and so outsiders who have to firstly be paid and secondly are not seen as trustworthy as family members, are not taken in until the business grows to a point where there is no alternative, or the outsiders have special skills which are absolutely essential. Even then it is often a family member who will be set to overlook the professional to ensure that all remains well. It is interesting to note from a socio-religious cultural angle that the professionals who are hired at this stage will almost always be from the religious-cultural group that the business family belongs to. To trust a complete 'outsider' is usually very difficult at this stage.

The long and short of this is that generations are mixed at any given point and the relationships very complex. Roles of family members are most often not clearly demarcated and shift as the need arises, which adds to the complexity. Consequently there is a differing sense of contribution on the part of each person which in the absence of a formal performance appraisal system leads to a lot of internal politics at the time of any transition of power. Despite all that I have said, the founder's equation is different.

The issues are not of authority alone. They have to do with respect, inspiration, loyalty and commitment. The founder's equation is different. The anxiety, even fear of failure at startup, the need to 'show' the world what you can do, produce a level of energy that is hard to replicate later. His successor's challenge is to continue the inspiration and commitment at startup without the factors that differentiate startups from businesses which are now past the startup phase. In the second and third generations this is an even bigger challenge. To fight complacency, a sense of 'we have arrived', an unspoken belief that nothing more needs to be done, since the business is obviously successful.

An excellent example of how to continue this drive is from the life of Sam Walton, the legendary founder of what may well be called 'the most successful business on earth', Wal-Mart. In the 1960's, he was in his 40's and had 15 stores and was independently wealthy. Most normal entrepreneurs would have relaxed and spent their time running their businesses trying to 'consolidate' them and making provisions for their families. Sam on the other hand saw the future which lay in discounting and reinvented his business with two principles: Lowest cost for the customer and highest growth for Wal-Mart.

This meant rethinking his entire business model which like any normal business was focused on earning the highest possible margin on sale. He turned this thinking on its head and decided that Wal-Mart would cut margins to the bone. Now that put two major challenges before him and his team: reduce his own cost in every possible way and increase his sale volume to grow his profits by volume and not margins. As I mentioned earlier, Sam Walton would fly low over country towns, triangulate on likely intersections and buy a piece of farmland. Then his people would build a store there as quickly and smoothly as rolling out a carpet. Today (2007) Wal-Mart has 6500 stores in 14 markets, with 1.9 million associates servicing 179 million customers annually. It is true that some cracks seem to be showing today, especially in terms of employee turnover but the logic of the business model: lowest cost to customer, fastest growth of volume: still holds good and is the mantra of discounting retail business. Wal-Mart used technology to create just-in-time deliveries. It used technology to make inventory control a fine art where store managers know their to-the-minute stock and by a combination of hard negotiating with suppliers, superior delivery process and a database second only to the Pentagon, manage to keep growing their business even during an economic slump.

Defining 4 Critical Parameters

There are 4 critical parameters that any family business that wishes to transform itself from being person-led to becoming process-driven, must define. It is essential that all these parameters are clearly thought out, defined and the criteria made public. It is the lack of clear definitions that leads to claims of nepotism from one branch of the family and discrimination from another. When these four parameters are clear, it preempts a lot of internal conflict and clears the muddy waters and promotes transparency in all dealings.

1. **Entry:** What does it take to enter the business?
2. **Progress:** How is success measured and rewarded?
3. **Succession:** How is succession determined?
4. **Exit:** On what conditions can a family member be asked to leave the business?

What does it take to enter the business?

Business success is a skill, not a hereditary trait.
Ask, "Is our business an aspirational place for high potential employees who have multiple choices? Or a parking lot for those who have no choice? Do young professionals in various disciplines who are wooed on campus by major corporations

choose your company over others?" GE for example has been 'Most Preferred Employer' for decades even though it is not in the top three salary payers in the United States. People join GE with the same state of mind as they go to Graduate School; to get training and experience which will enhance their market value. The working atmosphere, the collegiate partnership and the challenges that working for GE provides are so stimulating that most stay on, many for their entire careers, like Jack Welch did. Those who leave do so after making significant contribution and become ambassadors of GE worldwide. GE gets a huge amount of business from ex-GE people who are working in different companies. It is no accident that GE has provided the highest number of CEOs to American business. Ask, "What value do we add to those who work for us?" That is the key to attracting and retaining the kind of talent that you need achieve your goals. Like most things this is not an accident. Success is never an accident. It is the result of planned, intelligent effort.

So what makes a business an 'aspirational place'?
Firstly it is rigorous, even tough, entry criteria but which are surmountable and surmounting which is a credit in itself. Universities that are difficult to get into are the most sought after because if one succeeds in getting in, then that itself is a measure of the person's worth. The same applies to businesses.

About Merck they say that to work at Merck is like working in one of the finest research academies in the world. Merck publishes the names of its scientists in its promotional material and scientists sit on the board. Many young people have read the books these people have written and the opportunity to work alongside one of them is something that they would gladly give an arm and a leg for. Who is it who works for you that is an icon in the market that young people would aspire to work for?

The entry criterion must depend on the job, not on the individual. Anyone who satisfies that criterion must be hired. The best must be selected whether or not he is a family member. If the family member is not the best among the applicants then he must not be hired, even though he and/or his parents are shareholders. The easiest way to understand this logic is to see what happens in a publicly held company. The owners are the shareholders. If one of them wants to work for the company, she applies and is hired if she is found to be competent. If not, she does not get the job even though she is a shareholder and therefore a part owner of the company. As a shareholder of IBM for example, you can't just walk into the company and say, "Excuse me, I have decided to work here from today and I will call myself Director Marketing." That in effect is what happens with sons and daughters of the family in a family business and this is as foolish and ridiculous as the example above.

Hiring right means to hire people who have the attitude, skills and experience that the vacancy demands, not on how many shares they own. Sensible shareholders want the company to do well as that is the only way their stake becomes more valuable. They will never agree to someone being put in charge of the company just because they just inherited a large chunk of shares from their father. The same logic must be applied to family businesses. Shareholding is not a reason for hiring or handing over control. For example, anyone can buy a car, but to drive it, you have to learn how. If someone does not know how to drive but starts to drive just because he just bought a car, they will not get very far intact. All this logic is so easy to understand, yet we see family after family which inducts young well meaning but inexperienced and incapable sons and daughters into the business as if just being born into the family makes them experts in how to run the business. It is important to remember that running a business well is a matter of 'jeans and not genes' – hard work and not an accident of birth.

Secondly ask, "What value do we add to our employees? By working with us how do our employees become more valuable in the market? What makes them superior to those who have never worked for us? What is the value of our name on their CV?" GE hires on the basis of its training programs. It projects them as the reason why people should want to work in GE and they are the reason people want to join GE. To enhance their own market value. The GE name on the CV is money in the bank.

They know that working with GE for 5 years adds more value to them than working with a much higher paying employer for the same period. It is true that some leave. But it is equally true that others stay on and become a Jack Welch. Some family businesses ask the question, "What is the use of training employees because when they get trained they leave?" I answer by quoting Zig Ziglar: 'What is worse than training people and losing them? Not training and retaining them.'

If you add value to people, you become an aspirational place to work in. If not you are a stopgap at best. As you add value to them, they add value to you and in the end everyone benefits. But if you change this rule for family members, then you actually lower the entire image of being an aspirational place. After all who wants to work hard and join a place when you know that the boss's son can and will become your boss, no matter what you do?

Entry criteria for family members
Who can enter? How must they enter? What must they do to prove themselves worthy?

The first challenge is to set entry criteria for family members to enter into the business. In most families it is a default setting that all male members will enter the business. In some countries youngsters in business families seem to be allergic to education and enter the business immediately after leaving high school. Given that they are youngsters with little maturity and often an inflated sense of self importance, the results are not pleasant or useful for anyone, least of all for the youngsters themselves. Some families are more mature in this.

They insist that the youngster first finishes his tertiary education and then joins. In my view the best way to ensure that you get the best is to do the following:

1. Change the default setting and make a job in the family business an aspirational achievement that has to be won not merely inherited. Make it clear from the outset that the family and the business are two different things. That though family members will naturally enjoy their share of profits as shareholders but for those same profits to keep accruing the business has to be managed well. That is a skill, not a genetic factor. So only those who can prove that they are ready to contribute can enter the business.

2. For that they need to be able to do two things: the same as anyone else who wants to be hired: get a great education

and get some good worthwhile experience in some good place. Insist that the scion of the family goes to a top notch college and gets a great specialist education. Let him stand on his own feet for that. Don't buy the seat for him. While he is there don't give him any preferential treatment. Let him stay in the regular college hostel and go around on a bicycle or whatever is the norm with other students. That way he will learn social skills and make some good friends along the way. Many rich fathers give their sons their own apartments and buy them expensive cars and then wonder why the kid fails in the exams.

3. Keep a tight control on all expenses and focus on studies and hard work. Nobody ever died from working hard and neither will your beloved child. Remember that he has to return and inspire respect. Nobody respects a soft little pussycat that couldn't make it on its own without holding its father's hand.

4. Once his education is over, let him join the biggest, meanest, leanest and toughest multi-national in the world and work for 5 years. 7-10 years is even better. That is the minimum time needed to get some worthwhile experience and learn the business. He will still be under 30 when he comes back. This will give him an idea of market competition, give him a standing on his own merit and if he is smart he will be able to pick up some neat tricks on the way. This way he will get a real-time international experiential education at no expense to you. He will also build a network that will come in very handy later in life when he is working in your company. Once

he has his experience then invite him back. Don't force. Invite. If he does not accept immediately then he is the one you want. Then induct him into the company and give him some real freedom and responsibility.

5. Another even better way is to challenge him to start a new business. Let him present a business plan to you. Offer to finance him and then help him if he needs any help. If he succeeds you just helped create some more business for your family. If he fails, well that is the fee for his education. Analyze the learning; ensure he learned his lesson and ask him to give you a new business plan.

Family Leadership Boot camp – Training youngsters

"The dictionary is the only place where success comes before work."
Vince Lombardi

What it takes to be Number One
The famous address of Vince Lombardi –

"Winning is not a sometime thing: it's an all-the-time-thing. You don't win once in a while, you don't do thing right once in a while, you do them right all the time. **Winning is a habit***. Unfortunately, so is losing....*
It's a reality of life that men are competitive and most competitive games draw the most competitive men. That is why they're there – to compete. They know the rules and objectives when they get in the game. The objective is to win – fairly, squarely, decently, by the rules – but to win. And in truth, I've never known a man worth his salt who, in the long run, deep down in his heart, didn't appreciate the grind, the discipline.

There is something in good men that really yearns for, needs, discipline and the hard reality of head-to-head combat.

I don't say these things because I believe in the brute nature of man or that men must be brutalized to be combative. I believe in God, and I believe in human decency. But I firmly believe that any man's finest hour- his greatest fulfillment to all he holds dear – is that moment when he has worked his heart out in a good cause and lies exhausted on the field of battle – VICTORIOUS."

Vincent Thomas Lombardi (June 11, 1913 – September 3, 1970) was an American football coach. He was the head coach of the Green Bay Packers of the NFL from 1959-67, winning five league championships during his 9 years.

While the youngsters are studying let them get summer jobs in your business and let them start at the bottom. If you are in the shoe business this means sitting on footstools and helping customers try on shoes. Not sitting at the cash register or simply walking the floor ordering others about. If you are in the restaurant business, this means swabbing the floor and working in the kitchen and eating with the staff, what they eat. No meals sent from home by Mommy. If you are in the retailing business this means hitting the road selling stuff and learning all about supply chain management by walking the street, not sitting in an air-conditioned classroom in a fancy business school or driving around in the BMW that you gave him for his birthday. If you are in the manufacturing business this means lying on his back with the grease-ball greasing machinery on a Sunday which is the maintenance day. No, your son does not get the day off to go watch football just because his father owns the place or the football team. If you are interested in continuing to own the place and the football team then you need successors who understand how the place runs. That's why the rigor.

The biggest challenge for the founder is to build the character of the children and for that, many times, kindness comes packaged in steel armor. Even eagles need a push, as the title of the book says, and if you want him to fly you need to be prepared to kick him out of the nest. The wings gain strength only from flapping desperately to stay in the air. Yes he will fall. How else can he learn how to land? Then he will fly again. For success is nothing more than this: To rise every time you fall.

How is success measured and rewarded?
Success is not a matter of opinion. It is a measurable fact.
The credibility of any measurement is in its uniformity. Only if everyone is measured on the same standard does the standard become trustworthy. If you have one standard for employees and a <u>lower</u> standard for family members, then you are only lowering the dignity of your own family. People don't respect those they consider less than themselves. And that is what family members will become if they are rewarded according to a less exacting and rigorous standard of measurement. I am amazed at the number of family business people who actually recommend that family members should have lower standards than professionals that the family employs. I can only assume that they are not thinking when they say these things. For how anyone with even a single digit IQ can say something like this is beyond me. When family members succeed on the same standard as everyone else they acquire high prestige and people will willingly follow them when they become leaders. Create a performance culture of measuring results. Everyone and everything should be measured and the family must set the example. If I had my way, I would set higher

standards for family members that for outsiders. My logic is that this is precisely what the original founder did. The founder earned respect because he was clearly superior. Why anyone imagines that this logic changes from the 2nd generation onwards is something I can't understand.

It is essential to ensure that everyone is measured on the same standard. A rigorous and objective performance appraisal system is essential. In principle this consists of goal setting by mutual dialogue at the beginning of the year. Followed by ongoing measurement as the year progresses. And then assessment and reward at the end of the year. Making it a collaborative process enhances both transparency and trust and people feel empowered to know that they are working to achieve the goals that they set themselves. The feeling of being imposed on from above is eliminated and a high level of commitment is achieved. Rewards must be linked to contribution, in terms of annual bonuses and profit sharing schemes.

Annual increments must be uniform to take care of inflation. All rewards must be based on current contribution and in relation to it. Senior management including family members must be measured on how they add value to the vision, how they are able to reinvent strategies and how they display structured ways of risk taking. For family and top management this can be a done by peer rating on a 360° basis. This is not about passionate speeches in favor of grandiose schemes. It is about the rigor to convert a dream into a strategic plan that can convince critical peers to commit resources to it.

Merck has a system where if anyone has a business plan for which they need funds, they can present their scheme to their peers who can choose to commit to this scheme from their budgets, provided they are convinced about its feasibility. The Venture Capital Fund that I have suggested earlier for business families works on the same principle. Anyone who wants funds for a particular venture presents his/her plan to the Venture Capital Fund assessment team comprised of the top management of the organization and they can decide what to commit to it. This method of assessment ensures that performance is the key to success and drives home the message that anyone who delivers can succeed in the organization. It also gives those who decide to invest in the idea to become stake holders who can help the individual to succeed as well as benefit from their success.

It is important to differentiate between the dividend that family members receive as a result of the business doing well and individual performance based rewards. For performance rewards there must not be any differentiation between family and non-family professionals. Performance rewards are for performing. All those who perform and meet the criteria of success must get the same reward. As a family member the individual will also be entitled to whatever dividend the family gives its members at the end of the year. That has no bearing on his or her individual performance.

Career progress for family members
What must they do to progress in their careers? Is anything in this different from what professional managers must do?

Short answer: Yes.

It must be more difficult, the standards higher, the challenges more exacting because your child is an owner and so must be an example-setter. Also that is how he will gain respect in the system. Remember that ultimately the professionals will report to him and you want them to do that with pride, confidence and knowing that he knows the business better than they do. That way they will look up to him and not see him as being dependent on them. After all this is how the founder earned his own prestige and respect, by clearly being superior, inspirational and seen as someone who adds value to anyone who is fortunate enough to be associated with him. I have seen too many family businesses which would not last one week if key professionals walked away. And they know it and demand their pound of flesh which is willy-nilly given. I have even known where professionals have literally held owners to ransom as it were and then walked out and set up in competition.

This will never happen if you develop your family members such that each becomes an expert in his or her own right. Career progression must also be on the same terms as it is for other professionals with only one difference: the family member has the opportunity to sit on the Family Board one day. Opportunity, not certainty. Within the organization promotions must be need and merit based. Remember that a promotion is not a reward. It is an opportunity to do a job that is more complex and difficult and a great learning opportunity. So people who are promoted must be monitored and coached and supported.

How is succession determined?

The one who is best for the organization must succeed.
The only acceptable criterion for succession is to see who would be best for the organization. Not who is the oldest or any other

criterion. There are two essential mindsets that must be in place to ensure smooth succession.

1. The 'Family' depends on the business and needs the business.
2. Inside the business, the only factor for preference is contribution.

This is often the most difficult of decisions because it is an issue of power. In the desire to hold onto power people don't share information, resent being questioned on the performance of their businesses and generally act as if they were running personal fiefdoms. Like the GE airplane interview method for selecting successors, if you create a system where the superior will actually lose his job if he does not develop successors you will build a culture that enforces empowerment and subordinate development. Organizations where you need to persuade or force superiors to train subordinates or to delegate some powers are organizations with a ticking time clock waiting to be taken over.

Leaders who become indispensible are usually very poor at developing people. They take pride in the fact that the place can't run without them. Such people must be put on a monitoring plan to shape up or ship out. It is better to fire someone who will not develop others early in the game rather than be faced with a leadership vacuum when you actually need to hand over to successors. Show me a company where the CEO's job is threatened if he does not develop someone to take his place and I will show you a company which is well suited to outlasting its founders. This culture must be propagated strongly and seriously all down the line. Delegation and people development suffers because it is treated as a 'nice to do' rather than as a 'critical to personal success' issue. Where there is a reward for developing subordinates and a price to pay for those who don't you will find that people development is taken very seriously.

To encourage collaboration, create peer rating and reward performance. Openly sharing information, offering to help each other to succeed and shared responsibility for decision making are the keys both to business success as well to keep the family together and these must be institutionalized in the system and not left to anyone's individual inclinations. I have described how to do this later in this book where I have suggested several things that business families can do.

Exit: Terminating Family Members

This is a big one. Some people are of the opinion that family members can't be terminated under any but the most extreme circumstances like theft or doing something detrimental to the family. My view is that like performance bonuses, termination must also be linked to productivity. To allow the business to suffer losses because a family member is ineffective is to punish the whole family and all employees for the doings of one person. This is not only grossly unfair on everyone, but more importantly it vitiates the atmosphere of a results driven culture that we are trying to create. By such a policy we are at once undermining all claims to fair-play, justice and merit based career progression. So people who don't deliver must go; family or no family. Such people must not even be put in some other part of the business for the same reason – their presence will legitimize ineffective working. Also more than likely they will create their own politics, especially as they are family members which can lead to all sorts of undesirable results. When you decide to terminate, the best way is to do it as quickly and decisively as possible. A clean cut with a sharp knife is always better, cheaper and kinder. The individual remains a shareholder and part of the family. It is just that they no longer come to the office. As I have said earlier, owning a business and running a business are not the same.

Keeping the Business Family intact – 5 Key Structures

I have suggested 5 structures that are most beneficial in achieving our goal: Making the business process driven while keeping the family together.

The What-if Team
Dissent is the thing that most families fear the most. Interestingly dissent is the best glue to keep the family together, provided it is open and channeled in a positive direction. My suggestion is to

create 'What-If' Teams. Any group of people can form a 'What-if' team; family or non-family. Anyone who would like to challenge any existing process, issue, policy, method or system.

Three conditions must be set for this:
1. Announce the formation of the **WHAT-IF** team and define the issue that they plan to address and the people on it.
2. The current issue must be thoroughly analyzed and presented to its current sponsors who must agree that the **WHAT-IF** team has clearly understood the status quo.
3. The **WHAT-IF** team must present their critique and complete the presentation with an alternate method which is in some way better.

The purpose of this structure is to encourage a culture of open sharing of thoughts, ideas, and disagreements with a focus on problem solving. Not merely on criticizing, complaining or fault finding.

WHAT-IF teams are also excellent tools to use for scenario planning. Scenario Planning is a very powerful tool to make strategic plans for the future. It consists of imagining a set of circumstances and then extrapolating the possible consequences if some of the critical parameters in the circumstances changed. For example, the change in currency value, commodity prices, price of raw material, cost of transportation due to increase in oil price, wars, social unrest and so on. **WHAT-IF** teams can prepare alternative scenarios and suggest ways for families to deal with such situations when and if they arise. This becomes a major competitive advantage when the eventuality happens because being prepared is half the battle won. Such exercises are also excellent preparation for leadership in the organization for those who take the initiative to volunteer and this can be an informal leadership selection process to see who takes the initiative to volunteer on **WHAT-IF** teams.

There are 4 major benefits of this structure:

1. Dissent comes into the open and is handled at a logical, objective level, and not in an emotional, nebulous way. Internal politics does not start as there is no need for it. People are given the legitimacy and place to speak about anything that they don't like or want changed.
2. The message is clearly given that it is okay to want something changed as long as you can come up with a better way. If not, then you need to learn to live with the current way and keep working to come up with a better way.
3. The message is clearly given that the family is open to any change that can result in positives. That nobody is wedded to any idea as such. What is most important is what is best for the family.
4. Scenario planning helps the family deal with emerging challenges with foresight instead of having to get into a firefighting mode.

Council of Elders
This comprises of all those who are in the oldest surviving generation in the family irrespective of whether they are active in business or not. The main purpose of this structure is to ensure that the wisdom of experience is not lost. Neither is the influencing power of the elders and that this power comes out in the open and is used positively for the benefit of everyone. In my opinion, senior ladies of the family must also be invited to sit on this Council. Excluding women from the public influencing space,

as is done in many families, drives their influence 'underground' and starts all kinds of politics with the men becoming their mouthpieces in public. The effects are disastrous to say the least. It is far better to give them their due and acknowledge their support for the men to achieve what they have done and to open the space for those of them who have the initiative, education and training to contribute to the business in positive and powerful ways.

Leadership: The Council of Elders will have a leader for a period of one year. This position will go compulsorily by rotation to every member of the Council of Elders. So there is no need for any politicking or lobbying for leadership. This leadership by rotation also ensures that everyone will cooperate with everyone else and no single branch of the family overshadows the others.

Decision making: Will be by a process of consensus. This is defined as: everyone gives their opinion with data and their logic for arriving at their suggestion. Then the leader will make the decision and everyone abides by and supports it. This eliminates the sometimes protracted debates when consensus (meaning that everyone must agree) is used as a decision making tool. The leader has the option of nominating someone else to take the decision instead of himself. This is because that person may have some special knowledge or training or because that person is the key stakeholder in the outcome. However the rule is that once the decision is taken, everyone supports it and abides by it as if it was their own.

Scope: The scope of operation of the Council of Elders will extend to all family matters, business or personal. The Council may choose to delegate certain matters to other bodies. For example a key business decision may be referred to the Executive Council with a request to give their recommendation. Or for a marriage a sub-committee of aunts may be asked to make enquiries and recommend a course of action. The final authority of sanctioning in favor of or against the decision remains the responsibility of the Council of Elders.

Young Leaders Council

The Young Leader's Council's primary role is to meet periodically and deliberate on emerging opportunities and create strategies to take advantage of them. Non-family professionals may also be included on this Council for the knowledge & skills they may bring to the table. The Young Leader's Council may also choose to form **WHAT-IF** teams to plan scenarios or to propose policy changes. These proposals can be presented to the Executive Council periodically. Some of them may be recommended to the Venture Capital Fund as the case may be.

When dealing with such proposals the Executive Council must follow the following rule:

1. Say Yes! Most of the time. Monitor this quarterly.
2. When you say No – give reasons.
3. You can ask for more information, but put a timeline on when you will give a decision and stick to it.

Under no circumstances must proposals be left hanging in the air without a decision nor must they be shot down without legitimate reasons openly shared with the proposers. Nothing kills enthusiasm faster than leaving things pending without a decision or simply killing an idea autocratically. The main purpose of the Young Leaders Council is to give the younger generation hands-on training in actual, live decision making. This won't happen if they are not allowed to do things on their own. The purpose of putting the condition of approval by the Executive Council is to hedge the risk but it is not meant to become a roadblock to risk taking or new ideas, simply because the elders have become too risk averse. That is why the condition of giving reasons for declining. This also shows respect and appreciation for the enthusiasm of the younger generation and keeps the hope alive that as long as they come up with good ideas with detailed implementation plans, they will get the support of the Elders.

Idea generation must be a regular programmed activity and not left simply to the hope that an idea may come along in due course. Ideas are needed all the time and their generation must be guaranteed. When the presenter can see a clear benefit in presenting an idea in that if it is accepted then he may well have the opportunity to guide it to fruition, people become very enthusiastic about generating new ideas and innovating. The benefit of programming activity is that if ideas have not come by the time the scheduled meeting comes along this puts pressure on people to generate ideas.

One of the biggest dangers in business as indeed in all of life is complacency. When the sense of urgency disappears and complacency sets in it is a danger signal of impending demise. Unfortunately by its very nature it happens in a state of low awareness and so goes unnoticed until it is too late. Like programmed obsolescence which ensures new development, programmed innovation is a powerful tool to ensure that the fresh breeze of new ideas flows in regularly to blow away the cobwebs of conventional wisdom. Who better than the young blood in the organization, to create this breeze because they are the future on which the family depends anyway?

The Young Leaders Council gives the young leaders in the organization a chance to exercise their own creativity and demonstrate initiative. This Council can also be a group resource to which others can come for any help that they may need. It may form special task forces for innovation, corporate governance, and so on and be a shared resource for the whole company. One of the strategies of the Young Leaders Council can be to explore new business opportunities in non-traditional areas or countries. This can result in one or more of the young leaders becoming the founders of a new business in the new place.

That would be a leveraged opportunity for the young person and a new area of expansion for the main business. In GE as a part of the Executive Development Program, a top management program with business leaders that Crotonville runs, teams are sent out to various countries to scout for business opportunities. They return and present business plans. Proposals which are accepted result in serious support for such projects which has been the beginning of GE's presence in several countries.

Eligibility Criteria: All the younger members of the family who have completed their undergraduate education will be eligible for appointment to the Young Leader's Council. Those who can satisfy the entry criteria will be appointed to the Council. The admission criteria will be:
1. Track record till date including academic excellence. You don't need losers.
2. Demonstrated leadership till date including social and community work.

3. Peer assessment: Aspirant must have a sponsor and a seconder on the Young Leader's Council who are not directly related to him/her.
4. Consensus Ballot: Everyone on the Council must agree to the new entrant's membership. Where there is disagreement, there will be open dialogue in the presence of the incumbent.
5. Panel interview: An interview by a panel consisting of members from the Council of Elders, Executive Council and Young Leader's Council in the proportion 2:2:2.

Leadership: Leadership of the Council will be by rotation but the period may be varied depending on the number of members because one year may be too long for people to have a realistic chance at leadership.

Retirement: Young Leaders Council members will come up for retirement every 3 years and will be eligible for re-election. This will ensure that the membership has aspirational value and is not seen as something that they have to do nothing to gain or retain. Members who have not done anything in their tenure may not be re-elected and those who do, may get multiple terms. It also institutes the concept that family participation in leadership positions is not automatic and must be earned. At age 45 members will retire permanently from the Young Leaders Council.

The Arbitration Council

Many, if not most business families break up, not because their issues of conflict are in fact so intractable, but because there is often no pre-set conflict resolution process in place. I believe that a conflict resolution process is absolutely essential to the survival of the family as one unit. Actually in most families as long as the founder is alive, he does the arbitration. In the old social order, the oldest uncles and in some cases the oldest of the cousins inherited this mantle. In some cases it is the mother or oldest aunt who plays this role. However all these are highly informal, indefinite roles which have the authority of tradition but last only as long as people are true to tradition. In our changing times, I believe it is essential to create a system that will perpetuate independently of any individual's personal authority.

Structure: The Arbitration Council must have an odd number of members, not exceeding 5. These must be uncles and cousins elected by secret ballot by all the family. They will remain on the Arbitration Council until one of them volunteers to retire or dies. In that case his/her place will be filled by another ballot. At least 2 out of the 5 or 1 out of 3 should be of different genders. It is essential to have women on this council because without their active participation I believe such a council will be doomed. For some families this may need some fundamental changes in their way of thinking. Women influence anyway. Putting them in the driver's seat ensures that the influence is in the best interest of the entire family.

Leadership: The Arbitration Council will have a head with a term of one year to change by rotation. This person will be the final spokesperson for the Council and will be the Convener of all proceedings.

Working Method: When a dispute arises it will be brought before the Arbitration Council. The head of the Council will call for a meeting in which the following process will be followed:

1. Listen to the all the parties concerned and compare notes without coming to any decision individually.
2. Attempt to bring about conciliation by individual counseling as the case may warrant.
3. Consult independent legal counsel if required or gather more information if that is necessary.
4. Decide by a process of consensus with the proviso that everyone must agree to the decision.

The Arbitration Council will exist in suspended animation and will come into operation only when some matter is brought before it. Everyone in the family must know that it is there for them if they need it and what to do to invoke it.

Ethos: It is essential to understand that to be selected by the family to sit on the Arbitration Council, is the highest honor that the family can bestow on any member. The prestige, credibility and effectiveness of the Council will depend on the amount of trust that it inspires. Therefore it is absolutely critical that it always remains and is seen as completely neutral, objective and trustworthy. Nothing must ever be done by any of the Council members that can be construed as being partial to anyone. It is not only important that justice is done but that it is seen to be done. No confidence of anyone should ever be betrayed. Nothing must be done that will cause the constituents to lose confidence in the Council. If they lose confidence in the Council they will lose confidence in the process itself. Being on the Arbitration Council is a high honor and with it comes high responsibility.

Mentoring Network

The single most important requirement for any business family is to develop its second line. In almost every family that I consult with I have heard the same complaints: "They don't take responsibility or initiative!" and "They don't let us do anything or take any decision." When these statements come from 65-70 about 35-40 year olds and vice versa they are no longer funny.

As I have written in detail earlier you learn how to do business by doing business. Not by reading books or watching others do business. However in the urgency of daily transactions despite the best intentions, not everyone gets the same opportunities to learn. So it is necessary to set up a formal training system where to the extent possible, all cousins get the same basic exposure and opportunities. Then when the time comes the best and most competent ones can be selected to fill any positions.

The best way to do this is to create a mentoring network and 'apprentice' one or more cousins to each uncle, senior cousin or key professional. Where the nature of the business permits, the apprentice can choose the area he/she wants to work in. The apprenticeship will consist of observation, conversations, presenting learnings, opportunities to take decisions, analyzing of decisions, special projects and an annual presentation by the mentor and mentee to the Executive Council. This will give the business leadership a chance to see how the mentees are developing as well as give the mentees exposure to the Top Management of the business. This will also be a de facto assessment of the mentoring skills of the seniors and lends a high degree of seriousness to the entire process.

Fringe Benefits
Apart from all the direct benefits of the structures that I have mentioned about, I believe that the following fringe benefits will also accrue:

Team working Skills: By creating formal spaces and structures for people to work together, share responsibility and take decisions the systems that I have suggested empower and support team working. This in itself becomes a very strong glue to keep the family together. It also prevents blaming, fault finding and criticizing. Instead it gets people to work together to solve problems and share learnings. Lasting bonds are formed between cousins and uncles and communication improves especially with the Mentoring Network as people are 'compelled' to work together.

Conflict Resolutions Skills: Both as a consequence of the Arbitration Council as well as by working on the Family Council (Council of Elders & Young Leaders Council) people will learn to resolve conflicts amicably. Among them some will develop a high degree of influence as facilitators and can be identified to serve on the Arbitration Council when required. The systems that I have suggested will prevent clique formation and isolating of anyone and will strongly encourage, even 'enforce' collaboration and mutual assistance.

Stronger relationships in the family & Bonding between generations: Perhaps the biggest benefit of all the structures that I have suggested, especially the Mentoring Network is strengthening of family relationships. Since the focus of every structure is the good of the whole family and not personal benefit to one or a group of individuals, the bonds between people develop strongly. Since family members must now work together and deliver on projects, they learn to support one another and to all pull in the same direction. They learn to collaborate and to build up their emotional bank balances which come in handy in times of stress.

WHEN 'FAMILY' MEANS SOMEONE ELSE

'Their's not to make reply,
Their's not to reason why,
Their's but to do and die:'

(Charge of the Light Brigade, by Alfred, Lord Tennyson)

Non-family Professionals in Family Businesses

The title of this chapter sounds melodramatic but when I was thinking about what to call this chapter, these lines from the famous narrative poem, 'The Charge of the Light Brigade' by Alfred, Lord Tennyson came to mind. Tennyson wrote "The Charge of the Light Brigade" in a few minutes on December 2, 1854, after reading an article in the London *Times* about the Battle of Balaclava in the Crimean War, which was fought from 1853 to 1856 between Russia on one side and England, France, Turkey, and Sardinia on the other. In the 10 years that I worked as a non-family professional in one of the oldest and most famous of India's family businesses, I have seen innumerable professionals who worked precisely as if these lines were their motto. I salute such loyalty for it is not easy to come by and not often appreciated. I remember one colleague of mine, who in 35 years of service (he was an accountant) sat in the same chair, at the same desk and gradually went grey. The chair took the shape of his body and the desk bore witness to the place where his hands rested as he worked, as the major part of his life passed him by. He did not become independently wealthy, he did not fulfill all his financial needs; he simply did his job.

1. So why do professionals join family businesses?
2. What should families look for in the professionals they hire?
3. What can you as the family business owner do to attract and keep the best professional talent?

These are the questions that I intend to address in this chapter. I trust that the learnings will be beneficial both to family business owners as well as professionals. Once again I would like to remind the reader that my canvas is the East, India, Middle East and Africa. Its cultural and social context and the way family businesses are run here. I say this because the more I see the way family businesses are run in the West and the more I read research on Western businesses (although most of it is generically titled: 'Family business') I am convinced that its cultural context should be clarified as being family business in the West. The differences are simply too stark. If the East and the West ever meet I believe it will be in the business world, but the time for that does not seem to have come yet.

Until then, 'The East is the East, and the West is the West; and the twain shall never meet.'

So why do professionals join family businesses?

It is inconceivable that any family no matter how gifted with numerous talented children will ever have a great enough variety of capable members to run a rapidly growing business. The more successful the business, the more rapid its growth, the more diverse the requirements of leadership, the more this maxim will prove to be true. Family businesses, like any other business, need a variety of skills and talents and need to hire professionals to fulfill those needs. Professionals, generally speaking and especially if they are hired from leading edge multinational process driven companies bring with them a global perspective, knowledge of highly effective business processes, cross national contacts and knowledge of how things are done in a non-family, process driven environment. All these things may not be written on their CV but are part of the package that you hire. More of this later as well as what happens to it once the professional enters the family system and what to do about that.

But why do highly qualified and experienced professionals join family businesses at all? Why do they leave a process driven multinational company and join a family business, sometimes at a lower pay package. I know a friend who took at 20% pay cut to leave a global MNC and join a large family business in India. And no, this was not a sign of mental aberration either. When I asked him he simply said to me, "I realized that in the last 6 months, I had not seen my children awake." There are many reasons why bright and highly competent professionals choose to work for family businesses over working for global MNCs.

One of the most common reasons that professionals join family businesses is to be close to the seat of power. It is the nature of the family business that key professionals get maximum exposure to the family. This is a source of satisfaction for many professionals for whom a personal touch is important. Being able to influence significant outcomes is more satisfying for some people than doing it themselves. Being king maker is more powerful than being king. In global MNCs actual personal contact with the CEO is rare indeed even for many senior managers. In a family business it is almost daily and at a close personal level.

Another common reason is generally a slower pace of life and more rational working hours. As technology becomes our slave-driver instead of being our servant, this is more and more true. Most managers who work for global MNCs in the East have superiors, key clients and even colleagues who live and work in the US or Europe. So conference calls which are ideally suited to their timing are the norm. That means the Indian manager has to be hooked onto his computer talking shop while all others about him are eating dinner or playing with their children or fast asleep. Yet next morning he has to be back in his office in India at 0830 like every one of them.

Of course it does not occur to him to ask why his American or European counterpart can't 'flex' his schedule to take a call during his dinner time. We are wired differently it seems, so to unquestioningly accept conditions which would have sent a Westerner ballistic is normal. But like everything else there is a breaking point at which the person says, "Enough is enough. I want to play with my kids. And if it means a pay cut, so be it."

Another reason is the traveling. Once again it is the Easterner working in the global MNC who does most of the travel. More so as travel has become more and more odious and less pleasurable with all the security considerations. 'Going abroad' which used to be a major reason why young professionals joined global MNCs soon wears out its novelty and becomes a drudge. It is not just common but an expectation and a norm that someone from India will take a non-stop or connecting flight to the US (18 – 20 hours), land in the middle of the night in his hotel and be ready to attend a meeting at 0800 am the next morning, bright eyed and bubbly and never mind the jetlag. I have done this myself enough to know from experience how much of a toll it can take on you. One does it for a while for a lot of reasons, but after that?? So people look for jobs where the only travel they will do is from home to office every day or at the most a couple of convenient domestic flights a month.

A fourth reason why a lot of Easterners choose family businesses over global MNCs is cultural. The family business is more homely, more in keeping with their own culture, more accepting of their cultural and religious observations and generally more 'human and friendly'. For example, in India or the Middle East or Africa, for a Muslim employee to go the masjid for the congregational prayer at midday on Friday, is not something that he even needs to ask permission for. It is expected, understood and accepted. I have had my Hindu colleagues remind me that it was getting close to prayer time and that I needed to leave the meeting that I was passionately involved in and go to the mosque. The meeting would be adjourned and the others would take their lunch break while I finished my prayer and returned. Nobody was inconvenienced and we all understood our priorities. Similarly in this part of the world it would not be necessary to explain why it is important to take a day off to attend the wedding of the daughter of their wife's cousin or the funeral of their mother in law's uncle. Everyone has the same concept of 'family' and everyone understands the importance of maintaining family relations. So another reason why professionals choose family businesses over MNCs is the greater understanding and acceptance of their personal cultural, religious and social behavior.

What should families look for in the professionals they hire?
There are 4 things that family businesses must look for when hiring professionals:

1. High degree of resonance with the values and cultural fit with the family:
This is perhaps the most important criterion for success. Without a very clear and good fit with the family's values and culture, the executive is unlikely to do well in the organization. There will likely be too many little causes for friction which coalesce into something more difficult to manage. It is therefore essential that at the hiring stage itself, the culture of the family and their values must be made abundantly clear to the incumbent. All too often we see situations where in the anxiety to hire a promising professional, the family glosses over details of their values which

become sources of much conflict later. Some family practices may also cause problems like professional managers having to be in attendance on family members when they travel to their areas. It is better to clarify such things.

I have mentioned this in the earlier chapter on Organizational Excellence but would like to reiterate here, that the Core Values of the organization must be absolutely sacred and sacrosanct with no compromise or qualifiers or exceptions to practicing them. Credibility falls through the gap between stated values and practiced values. These values must be made clear to the professionals right at the start and no exception must be made with respect to the action to be taken in case someone violates them, no matter how 'critical' that individual is supposed to be. The family must set the example in living the values and must not make an exception even with its own members.

I have personally witnessed the tragic collapse of morale and loss of credibility that happened, when in the case in point, two individuals were hired from outside at middle management level during the course of the turn-around of a company. Unfortunately they were totally corrupt, both financially and morally, but nothing was done to them because they were considered 'critical' to the turn-around process. The top management of the company chose to lose its own credibility and respect in the process. People who hugely respected the senior leadership started speaking against them and saw them as having lied to them all along when they used to say that integrity was inviolable and that corruption would be punished and that promotions would only be on the basis of demonstrated results. Some peers of these corrupt individuals and even some juniors complained about them to the top management and gave them abundant proof of their goings-on. But no action was taken. Instead the individuals in question started a vendetta against those who complained. Gradually the lesson was learnt, that the top management did not really mean what it said and that as long as commercial results were achieved, nothing else mattered. The result was that those who could not stomach the situation (the competent ones who also had a market value) left. Those who stayed, either simply bided their time, or themselves became corrupt and aided and abetted the corruptors.

The individuals in question became personally wealthy at the expense of the company. The entire culture of mutual respect and results based performance in the organization was destroyed in a matter of a couple of years. And the only people who were apparently blind to the change (or maybe they did not care) were the top management. To everyone else in the organization, what was happening was crystal clear. I am not sure if the owners thought this price worth whatever little profit they made, which could have been made in an honorable and decent way in any case. Values are only as good as they are practiced. Values not practiced are not worth the paper they are written on.

2. Previous experience working with the family's culture and in a family business

I believe this is an important element to look for when you hire non-family professionals. You may not always get it, but it is worth looking for. Family business dynamics need getting used to. If you hire someone who has worked for another family, then you save a lot of time and energy teaching a new person the ropes. Do a thorough reference check on the person you are hiring. Use your informal network. Talk to your mother in law's aunt, climb the grape vine. But find out what the earlier family has to say about the person you are hiring. If they are all delighted that you are thinking of hiring him, then think several times.

3. Experience working with a global multinational business and actual working knowledge of process driven systems and methods

One of the main reasons for hiring key professionals is for the knowledge that they can bring, especially of systems and processes. Professionals from leading edge global companies can become your benchmarks for service, efficiency and effectiveness. They can open doors for your company with key clients and constituents. They can become key influencers to create the kind of process oriented culture that you are trying to create. It is therefore essential that you are sure that you are getting what you need. Behavioral interviewing is a good way to ascertain if a professional can actually deliver what you need. Reference checking is again essential in this case as well.

4. Willingness to work at a level second to a family member (No 'need' to be CEO)

One last thing that is very important to be sure of when hiring key professionals is about their own career aspirations. In your family business, it is more than likely that the CEO's position is 'reserved' for a family member. This must be clear to the professional and he/she must find this acceptable. If a professional aspires to run his own show then he is not the right choice for you. Many professionals are willing to play mentor and facilitator to a family member. You will need such people to mentor your own successors and to create competence in the family. This is a very beneficial partnership.

What can you as the family business owner do to attract and keep the best professional talent?

There are some important things that Family Business Owners/CEO's must keep in mind so that they can create a climate that can attract and retain the best professional talent.

The first and foremost thing to do is to consciously make the decision to hire professionals. If professionals from big-name MNCs are hired as a matter of prestige or fashion as happens more often than one would like to believe, it is almost certain that the hire will go wrong. Once the conscious decision has been taken it is essential for the family to spend a sufficient amount of time helping the professional to understand what he or she is getting into. As I have mentioned in detail earlier, family business cultures are as different from each other as can be. The professional that the family business hires will more than likely not have any idea about the dynamics, culture, taboos, norms and accepted behaviors of the family and their business. It is likely that given the corporate MNC culture of a Western company, he may find some of the norms and expected behaviors difficult or even impossible to follow. In such cases it is better that this is discovered early and the hiring is not done, rather than have to go through what can be a painful and embarrassing termination. Be frank with the incumbent; let him see what and how you are from as close as possible. Share all that you do and expect him to do without reservation and then let him decide if he wants to join. It is a good idea also to create a space for his family to meet your family and share some mindscape. The social interaction can help in breaking the ice and helping both parties to see each other without any pretence, voluntary or otherwise.

Choose the best

Believe me; the best really want to work for you. Get professional help to hire the best because the best don't just happen round the corner. It is a common mistake that many family business owners make of treating professionals as a 'cost'. They hire below themselves as they don't want to pay what it takes to hire the best. This is a very costly mistake. And you will pay that price. It is an accepted fact in leading edge global MNCs that hiring superior people is the most cost effective choice. Survey after survey shows that superior people may be up to 15% more expensive but produce between 40-50% more in terms of output. Hire the best and from them, demand the best. Those who are worthy of their salt will welcome working to high standards. This will also create the kind of achievement oriented culture you need to attract the best talent. Many high profile professionals can attract capable people to come and work for them. People don't work for organizations; people work for other people. Having the right kind of professionals working for you will make your organization an aspirational place to work. Like attracts like. Winners attract winners. So do losers.

Treat them with respect
They are not the 'hired help'. They work for the company, not for you personally. Don't use them to do your personal jobs and actively discourage those who will offer to do them in order to suck-up to you. Give professionals responsibility that is commensurate with their qualifications so that you can really leverage their talent and experience for your company. Some family business CEOs collect professionals from various MNCs like people collect watches or paintings. Then they talk about who they have working for them. But when it comes to giving them freedom and authority to take decisions and really bring about change in the company, they tie their hands and don't allow them

to function. Professionals who have self respect and who are interested in their careers, leave when they see what is happening. Others, for their own personal reasons stay on, lose their edge and gradually vegetate at your expense.

Don't make promises you can't or won't keep
Treat them like the professional colleagues they are. Some business owners in their eagerness to hire some high profile professional promise them all kinds of things which they personally have no authority to deliver. When the promises don't pan out, the professional justifiably feels let down and will more than likely leave. I recall one case where one family business CEO hired a high profile HR head from a global MNC with the 'incentive' that the family wanted to replicate the global MNC's corporate university in India. The HR professional was very excited believed the dream merchant who hired him, only to be hugely disappointed later. He lasted with them for all of six months.

Pay well
This is a big one. Many family business owners are so used to doing things themselves or getting their family or friends to do things for them for love that they almost take umbrage if anyone suggests that service needs to be paid for in cash. When hiring professionals they treat having to pay a salary like having teeth extracted and try to haggle and pay as little as possible. On the other end of the spectrum are those who are over generous and pay out of guilt or in order to tell their friends how much they are paying key professionals. Both approaches are wrong. If you pay peanuts you get monkeys who will steal the peanuts. Honesty does have a price, believe it or not. And overpaying does not buy either loyalty or dedication. Check the market. Pay either the

market value or 5% -10% more, since your company may not be such a great name to have on the CV. But don't pay more than that. If the person you are hiring needs to be literally purchased then he is not worth hiring. You want people to join you also for the challenge and for what they think they can achieve for you.

Create a clear career path for them

Professionals are very anxious in family businesses to know where their career will take them. They may accept not becoming the CEO but they would naturally expect to get to the No.2 position or to the head of a functional or SBU role in a reasonable time. Create a career path for them based on clearly defined goals. I have recommended that even the CEO's job must be open to professionals because you want the CEO to be the best qualified person. And if it is a non-family person, so be it. That is good for the business and by inference good for the family.

Demand excellence

Demonstrate excellence. Inspire and then never settle for anything but the best. Competent professionals like to demonstrate what they can do. Set high goals and reward those who exceed them, handsomely. A good objective performance management system is also a major asset in attracting and retaining the right people. Many professionals are very apprehensive of subjective appraisals in family businesses and the whole business of being 'liked'. A clear-cut performance management system assures them that their achievements will be noticed and rewarded objectively and that their career progress does not depend on subjective likes and dislikes.

Expose them internationally: Invest in their learning

Give your key professionals international exposure. Let them publish, present papers at international seminars, teach at business schools, participate in service programs. Only if they meet others will they learn. What they learn they will bring back to you. Sure a couple will leave. Those couple would have left anyway. In any case you need a flow of a clean cool breeze, now and again. But others will join you because they see the caliber of people you have working with you. Make learning an item on the Performance Appraisal System. Provide learning opportunities, pay for them, and support those who learn. Then ask them how you can enable them to apply what they learnt in your place. Without the challenge of international exposure professionals will lose their edge and thereby their usefulness to you.

Don't be shortsighted with respect to employee development. People who want to learn are precisely the kind of people you need. Don't punish them for wanting to learn. Appreciate their spirit and support them, so that they will create a culture of learning in the organization. Some employers think differently, to their own detriment. One professional in a family business wanted to do an Executive MBA. His employer reluctantly agreed to give him leave without pay for the duration. The professional needed money to pay the fee which was quite hefty as he had managed to get admission to the topmost business school in the country. His employer refused to pay the fee and agreed to give him a loan for the amount and charged an interest of 8.33%. Finally his employer demanded that he sign a bond, not to leave their organization for a period of 3 years after his return. He signed the bond because he had no choice. But on the same day, he said to me, he also marked the date of termination of his job with that organization.

Give them a stake in the business
Key professionals help you to become more profitable. They are the cause of your well being. Acknowledge and appreciate that materially. Believe me, they are smart enough to know their own worth. They need to be appreciated and their contributions acknowledged. The best option is to give key executives a percentage of the profit. Some people recommend stock options or phantom stocks, but these can have other implications for the family itself. A percentage of the profit is a neat, clean way to give the professional a stake in the company without raising other issues. They get it if they deliver. Not unless.

Do's and Don'ts for professionals in family businesses?
When you decide to go to work for a family business, you may like to remember some things.

If values don't match nothing else will matter
Be very clear in your mind about your values and see if they match those of the Business Family. If they don't, waste no more time and look for another opportunity. If you join a family business which has values in conflict with yours, nothing else will matter for you. You will not do well and will almost certainly come to grief. Ask frank questions in the interview. Don't be shy to ask anything that you want to have clarified. The interview is also a good place for you to assess how you are likely to be treated once you join. Talk to people who know the family and do your own 'reference check' and have the good sense to listen to advice.

Don't play with your source of power
Remember that in a family business, ultimate authority lies with the family and therefore loyalty is the cardinal virtue. So never

play with the source of your power. That is a battle you can never win, because if you win, you lose and if you lose you lose anyway. Treat the family you are now working for, as your own. Be loyal to them. You owe it to them, because they are paying you well and giving you freedom to make a career for yourself. Be good to them. It is entirely likely that the family member you work with does not have your knowledge or experience. Remember that's the precise reason why you were hired; to teach the family, help them to become more competent and capable and build a great company. You were not hired to make them feel like fools. I am amazed at how many professionals forget this and go around telling the world what an ignoramus their boss (family member) is. Remember that you may call him ignorant, but he still owns the company and despite the fact that he does not have your degrees, he is the one who is paying your salary and probably has a personal net worth that is a 100 times your own. So he must have done something right, eh! Respect that talent, the risk taking that built the business and the capability that enabled him to hire you. If you were more capable than him, he would be working for you, not vice versa. Sure, you have some special expertise for which he hired you. Use it for his benefit, help him, guide him and respect him. Never talk behind his back because the world is round and what goes around, comes around. And then it bites, very hard.

Blood is thicker than water
Family is about the genes first. Family will always be family. No matter how many times you were invited to the CEO's home, you have not become a family member. No matter that the CEO asked you to 'think of himself as your father', it does not make you his son. His son will succeed him, not you. So if you are one of those who can't stomach that, then you are in the wrong place. Learn to

take satisfaction from being 'king maker' for you will never be 'king'. Guide the successor, train him, support him and protect him, for one day he will become your boss. And you can still have a great career.

After all if you worked for GE it is unlikely that you could realistically imagine that one day you would be the Chairman.

You work for the business, not for any family member
Don't offer to do personal things, even as a favor because this can be misconstrued and then lo and behold you will be seen as a lackey instead of a professional colleague. Don't fall into this trap. Always keep a respectful distance. Don't accept too many personal invitations and never loosen your hair too much no matter how much you are encouraged. Under no circumstances should you get involved in any family disputes. Don't talk about one family member to another. If a family member talks about any other member to you, listen if you must, but make no comments. Don't take sides because that is not your role. Never discuss the family with anyone. Especially in social circles. Treat the whole family as your client, not any individual member. Don't become a 'confidante'. That is not your role.

Trust does not come easy in family businesses. You will need to earn your trust the hard way. Most non-family professionals will be seen as a 'cost' and that too a 'necessary evil cost'. The onus to prove that you are a 'value buy' is on you. Beware of the founder's over involvement with detail. In many cases family members, especially founders, have a very close, even fierce sense of ownership of the business and does not see how his attention to detail can be seen as nitpicking by others. You will need to have a high degree of tolerance for such behavior and the tact to gently show the founder how he can safely delegate responsibility and hand it over to you. Confrontation does not work. Empathy, understanding and patience, does.

Never lose your edge
Remember that you were hired because of your competence and ability to deliver results. To maintain that edge you need to continuously invest in your own development. Never link your development to what the company can provide. Invest on your own and let your boss know what you are doing. Plan your own learning every year and track it. Ask for assignments where you can demonstrate your competence. Participate in international seminars and symposia. Publish and teach. Participate in training both as a learner as well as a teacher. Introduce innovative initiatives in the company and with the permission of your boss, make them public. Consciously work to facilitate the transformation from being person-led to process-driven. This will help you to create the kind of climate and culture that you will find personally stimulating. Become a coach and mentor to the family and guide the younger generation to become worthy successors.

Conclusion
Remember that the prestige of the company and the family is your prestige. Show gratitude and do good to them. If you do, you will find that it will come back to you in full measure. It is possible to have a very satisfying career in a family business provided you follow the rules of that world. They are different.

Acknowledgements & Concluding Notes

In this writing I would like to acknowledge the contribution of many people who patiently read the drafts and shared their comments. My erstwhile boss and friend, M. M. Venkatachalam (Venky Muthiah), my first family business client, CK Ranganathan (CavinKare), my colleague and dear friend on the Cranes Board, Ron Brown. I am grateful to my friend and erstwhile colleague Ram Bajekal, former CEO of Parry Agro who read the chapter on professionals in family businesses and shared his comments.

I am most grateful to Ebrahim Bhai Patel (Number One Enterprises) who believed in me and supported me in every possible way and opened the door to South African business for me. It is not possible for me to thank Ebrahim Bhai for all that he has done for me. I ask Allahﷻ to reward him in keeping with His Majesty.

I am most grateful to Ismail Kalla, Nizam Kalla (Amka Products). Ismail was the first one to have faith in what I was proposing and who gave me a platform to demonstrate my ideas. Nizam is a dear brother and friend whose whole family adopted my wife and me so that consulting with the Kalla family is more pleasure than work. Saleem, Hussein, Muhammad and their brothers; all my own family.
I am most grateful to Rafik Kassim, Hanif Yusoof and the Expolanka family and Tajudeen, Nizam and the Seapol family

who are implementing the ideas in this book in their organization. How can I describe the joy and profound gratitude that I experience as I see the Expolanka and Seapol top management reading my book and bringing alive before my eyes, the ideas that I have outlined in it. Thanks to them all, I have the rare privilege of seeing my dream come true before my eyes.

Most of all, I am profoundly grateful to my wife Samina for her everlasting patience and support of what I do. As she is not only a reader and critique but a living partner in all that I have written, her comments were most valuable. To all of them I am most grateful.

The thoughts in this book are not conclusive opinions. They are a sharing of what I learnt in the course of my own life, which may be of use to those who have their own businesses or are intending to start one and believe that they will benefit from a conceptualizing of the major people issues involved. I would be delighted if readers would exchange ideas and experiences with me on this subject.

I believe that businessmen and women as a group have the maximum potential to change the world that we live in. If we can influence them to change it for the better then we will all benefit. With these final thoughts, I wish all those who read this book, a long and exciting life of learning and business.

About the Author

Mirza Yawar Baig is the Founder of YAWAR BAIG & ASSOCIATES™. International Speaker, Author, Life Coach, Corporate Consultant, specializing in Leadership Development helping technical specialists transition into Management and Leadership roles. He helps Family Businesses make the critical transition from being 'Person-led to becoming Process-driven' and create robust systems that will enable the business to be handed from generation to generation. Yawar's book, **'The Business of Family Business'** shows business families how to grow, yet stay together, by drawing on his extensive consulting experience with both family businesses and multinational corporations. Yawar is a life coach and mentor for prominent family businesses in India, South Africa & Sri Lanka. His latest book, **'An Entrepreneur's Diary'** traces his own journey as an entrepreneur. Yawar specializes in helping Start-ups make the transition into their growth phase, helping them to look at challenges and take difficult critical decisions. In 28 years of training and consulting Yawar has taught more than 200,000 managers, administrators, teachers, technologists and clergy on 3 continents. He combines Eastern values with Western systems to transcend cultural boundaries. Yawar's style reflects openness, commitment to quality and value-based professionalism. Yawar speaks five languages. He writes blogs, articles and books on topics ranging from leadership to politics to Islam, focusing on applying learning to create models of excellence in local communities.

Yawar lives in Hyderabad, India and can be reached at www.yawarbaig.com or yawarbaig@gmail.com

Made in United States
North Haven, CT
16 November 2022